Plays from New River 2

Plays from New River 2

Feasting on Cardigans by Mark Eisman
Tiger in the Tree by M. Z. Ribalow
Baseball Game of the Week by James McLure

Plays from New River series
Edited by M. Z. Ribalow

McFarland & Company, Inc., Publishers
Jefferson, North Carolina, and London

Caution: *Feasting on Cardigans*, *Tiger in the Tree*, and *Baseball Game of the Week* are fully protected under copyright laws. Professionals and amateurs are subject to a royalty for all performances. All rights, including but not limited to professional, amateur, motion picture, recitation, lecturing, public reading, radio broadcasting, television, electronic and the rights of translation into foreign languages, are strictly reserved. All rights inquiries should be addressed to Rights Department, McFarland & Company, Inc., Box 611, Jefferson, North Carolina 28640.

Publisher's note: M.Z. (Meir) Ribalow died on August 23, 2012, after completing the manuscript for this book but before having an opportunity to read proofs (which task was completed by others).

LIBRARY OF CONGRESS CATALOGUING-IN-PUBLICATION DATA

Plays from New River 2 : Feasting on Cardigans / by Mark Eisman ; Tiger in the Tree / by M.Z. Ribalow ; Baseball Game of the Week / by James McLure ; Plays from New River series / Edited by M.Z. Ribalow.
    p. cm. — (Plays from New River series)

ISBN 978-0-7864-7275-8
softcover : acid free paper ∞

1. American drama—21st century. I. Ribalow, M.Z. (Meir Z.), editor of compilation. II. Eisman, Mark. Feasting on Cardigans. III. Ribalow, M.Z. (Meir Z.) Tiger in the Tree. IV. McLure, James. Baseball Game of the Week.
PS634.2.P66 2013
812'.608—dc23

                                2012040106

BRITISH LIBRARY CATALOGUING DATA ARE AVAILABLE

Feasting on Cardigans © Mark Eisman. All rights reserved
Tiger in the Tree © estate of M.Z. Ribalow. All rights reserved
Baseball Game of the Week © estate of James McLure. All rights reserved

No part of this book may be reproduced or transmitted in any form or by any means, electronic or mechanical, including photocopying or recording, or by any information storage and retrieval system, without permission in writing from the publisher.

Front cover: photograph of the New River © 2012 Scot Pope; masks and curtain images © 2013 Shutterstock

Manufactured in the United States of America

McFarland & Company, Inc., Publishers
   Box 611, Jefferson, North Carolina 28640
      www.mcfarlandpub.com

This volume is dedicated, by the publisher,
on the late Meir Ribalow's behalf,
to the talented individuals who hone their craft
with the New River Dramatists

Table of Contents

ACKNOWLEDGMENTS   viii

WHAT IS NEW RIVER?   1

NEW RIVER DRAMATISTS PLAY DEVELOPMENT PROCESS   7

INTRODUCTION   9

Feasting on Cardigans by Mark Eisman   11

Tiger in the Tree by M. Z. Ribalow   81

Baseball Game of the Week by James McLure   133

ABOUT THE PLAYWRIGHTS   191

Acknowledgments

Of the many people who have helped make the dream that is New River possible, several have helped in ways that were invaluable and unwavering. We could never have realized our creative haven without Dasha Shenkman, our International Chair, and Gayle Winston, our luminous and incomprehensibly generous host at River House. Wilton and Catherine Connor, John and Edie Crutcher, Robert Franklin, Jerry Heymann, Bud and Zanne Baker, Bruce and Jo Marie Lilly, John and Pam Anderson, Wallace Colvard and Tom Wilson, among others, have tirelessly given not only financial support but generously of their time, talents and unflagging efforts. Bill Baker was for years a one-man staff at New River. Leslie Carroll, in addition to her contributions as an actor, served as our pro bono literary manager and organized all the early work written at our sessions. Randell Haynes and Patricia Randell have both been not only core actors, but also tremendous resources with their extensive knowledge of actors and playwrights. Sam McGregor was always there when we needed her, and Spencer Humphrey provided redoubtable expertise. Thanks also to Matthew Wells, whose help has been invaluable and whose friendship is unwavering. The late and loved Jim McLure, a participating playwright, was supportive in so many other ways as well, and we will always miss him. Nothing we have done would have been possible without the support and preternatural understanding of Laura Woods.

What Is New River?

One evening in 1994 the phone rang in my Manhattan apartment. The caller identified himself as Mark Woods. He said I didn't know him, but that he had been speaking about an idea he had to Mark and Kay Ethridge, close mutual friends who lived, as he did, in Charlotte, North Carolina, and the Ethridges had immediately suggested that he call me. Woods said he wanted to schedule a phone conversation with me because, he explained, what he wished to discuss "would take some time." I said okay, and we agreed on a date to speak. Then I said: "Mark, before you hang up, why don't you give me some idea who you are and what in the world you're calling about." Four hours later, we were still talking passionately, and three things were already clear. First, we were kindred spirits. Second, that though we shared the same unusual ambition — establishing a creative Eden where talented writers could be nurtured and encouraged to raise the level of their storytelling to even greater heights — we were coming at it from very different yet complementary directions. He wanted to build it and I wanted to run it. And third, the Ethridges were right: Woods and I were a serendipitous professional match.

It took almost five years for Mark to find the perfect location for what we were then calling The Playwrights Project. It was at Healing Springs, in Ashe County, North Carolina, in the woods of the Blue Ridge Mountains, on the banks of the New River. Eventually, in honor of the river flowing past us and the new stream of creativity flowing from our writers, we re-named ourselves New River Dramatists.

Our first week, in March 1999, was unforgettable. We held our sessions in an abandoned schoolhouse which its owner allowed us to occupy both for that week and for the eight summers that followed. We stayed at River House, a jewel of a country inn two miles down the road, owned and run by Gayle Winston, a wonderful, wildly supportive angel (and famed chef, to boot) whom we soon referred to as the Goddess of Grassy Creek (where River House was officially located).

While Mark spent every waking hour trying to garner support for our endeavor, I established a structure for the work itself. We had a dozen seats at the table (both by artistic preference and financial limitations) and I invited four writers and eight actors to participate in reading, critiquing and developing the writers' work (as time passed, that evolved into five writers and seven actors, allowing some flexibility in those cases where an artist was both). The writers had mornings and nights to write. After lunch, we would all gather to read and discuss plays for four to six hours five to six afternoons a week.

Our process is much unchanged to this day (the table rules follow this piece). I'd been confident it would work, because much of my life — creating literary departments and theatre companies, and as a professional reader and writer of plays and screenplays — had been an unwitting preparation for just such an enterprise.

But when we gathered that first week in March 1999, my confidence in this process was unsupported by hard evidence. Ten years later, when we gathered for another week in March 2009, this time at River House itself, to commemorate and celebrate our first ten years, the resulting statistics were difficult to argue with. We had supported the work of some 70 playwrights who in turn had developed some 345 plays and screenplays, close to half of which had been either produced or optioned. Their work had been presented at major theatres around the world, and our writers had been awarded a cornucopia of literary prizes, including the National Book Award, the Simonovitch Prize, the August Wilson Award, and the National Medal of the Arts.

The key to our process is that New River does not produce. Ever. (We don't encumber, either.) This means all our attention is on encouraging the development of the work, not getting it ready for public display next Tuesday. We don't care if a writer works on a different project every time he brings one in, or changes her mind just before the session. We don't care if they finish a piece, or start three new ones. We're not producing plays; we're nurturing gifted writers so that their work, already fine, may be better than it would otherwise have been. Mark and I agreed early on that we wanted to pay each of the artists $500 per week, in addition to room, board and transportation, because it was so important to make pellucid our respect for their talents.

At New River, comments must address what the writer is trying to write, not what anyone else thinks he or she *should* write. Our first summer, Cassandra Medley, a terrific writer who happens to be an African-American woman, was writing a play about a "lily" (a black woman so light-skinned she passes easily as white) in 1957 Detroit. Zena is married to Brian, a white auto executive who has no idea she is other than a southern belle. Cassandra would bring in two or three scenes every other day, and the comments would raise questions that helped her continue to write it the way she wanted to. At the end of the first week, she had the entire first act, so we read it all to see how it sounded so far.

We ask writers to be silent during the initial round of comments, so as to quell potential defensiveness and have them listen instead to what everyone thought they heard. I refrained from commenting; the moderator has a greater value listening to what everyone else has to say, then synthesizing the major points that seem to keep occurring before inviting direct questions as well as further comments, during which time the writer can say whatever she (or he) wants.

When the first wave of comments was completed, I said to Cassandra: "I've heard eight comments which superficially sounded as if they were about different points, but they're really all tributaries of the same stream. And that stream is an uncertainty on the part of the audience as to how much she does or doesn't love Brian."

She interrupted me with, "No, she does love him, she really does."

To which I said, "If she loves him, that's fine with me; it's your play. If she doesn't love him, that's also fine with me; it's your play. But that's eight people that don't know one way or the other. There are only twelve of us in the room, and two of the remaining four are you and me. So whatever Zena feels about him, it isn't clear, is it, Cass?"

While she laughed, I continued, "And if you do want her to love him — since that's what you just said — you need to bring him into the play, because he clearly isn't there yet. *We* don't have to love him; we just need to believe that *she* does."

By the time she had completed the play, Cassandra had the entire room caring about Brian. And by developing Brian she also strengthened Zena, because now it *mattered* whether she stayed with him or not.

As crucial as we feel it is to help writers question, clarify and improve their work, we regard it as equally critical to encourage writers to write not what they are told might be most saleable, but what they know in their souls will be most true to their gifts: to write not for Caesar, but rather for God and the Unknown Friend.

James McLure, an experienced and much-lauded playwright, was working one summer on a two-character piece that seemed to me clearly an attempt to write something slick rather than from the *kishkes*. One night I asked him: was this the play he truly wanted, in his heart of hearts, to write? If so, I assured him, he would have our total support. But I wondered if he had really come to our mountain retreat to write this.

Well, no, he admitted. But there was really no point in writing the play he really wanted to write.

Why not? I asked.

Because, he said, there were 24 characters in it, and no one would ever produce it.

Good, I said. Write that one.

Really?

Sure. If you don't write it here, you never will. And if you do write it here, you'll be able to hear it. We can double or triple roles if need be, and we cast without regard to gender, age or race anyway.

But no one will produce it, he repeated, so what was the point?

Look at it this way. If you write the two-hander, in all likelihood no one will produce that one either, right?

He agreed wryly.

So no matter what you write, no one will do it anyway. So why not write the play your heart is in? That way, when they reject it, at least they'll be turning down what you really wanted to say.

That made sense to him, and he decided to write the large, intense piece that became *Blue Silence*, about a universe of good (not to be confused with honest) cops. The room had a great time developing it, because of its heartfelt passion and intelligence. Ironically, of the forty plays to emerge from New River that summer, *Blue Silence* became the first to be fully produced (in Los Angeles).

So that's our mission: to find the best writers we can and relentlessly encourage them to write whatever is truest and most important to them. Of course, to do this means constructing a creative community with considerable thought and care. If we have five writers and seven actors, we make sure the writers (as well as the actors) have a certain diversity: women and men, veterans and new writers, different backgrounds, ethnicities — as much of a balance as we can manage while making sure each writer is someone in whose talent we passionately believe.

With actors, we search for an unusual combination of characteristics. When you're casting a production of a play in New York, you go for the best actor available, and don't worry whether they go home at night and perform odd religious rituals while speaking in tongues. But in a community like New River where everyone is basically living together while working on an extraordinary variety of writing styles and subjects, the demands are different. Outstanding talent is of course a *sine qua non*, but we also need actors of extraordinary range, for they have to read an exceptionally wide variety of roles. They must possess keen intelligence, so that they can make helpful comments in a supportive fashion; be articulate enough to express their thoughts with cogent incisiveness; and be ensemble-minded enough to leave their egos at home.

The success of New River is based on how much the writers and actors inspire each other (we change some participants each week, so that no two weeks are ever exactly the same mix of artists). Many writers have remarked on how helpful this process has been. Jack Heifner, playwright of *Vanities*, calls our process "probably the most positive feedback I've had of my work in the 25 years I've been writing in the theater." Sharon Pomerantz, now known for her novel *Rich Boy*, says, "We felt lifted to a place of honor, as if the very fabric of society depended on what we were doing ... and it does." Denis Johnson, who subsequently won the National Book Award for *Tree of Smoke*, tells us, "I learned lessons I'll always treasure — the experience changed me." And Pulitzer laureate N. Scott Momaday simply says, "If I could spend a month in a place like this, I could write something REALLY good."

Now you know what some of the playwrights think of New River. But don't take their word — or ours. Read these three plays. See for yourself.

M. Z. Ribalow • Artistic Director • New River Dramatists

New River Dramatists Play Development Process

TABLE RULES

Read the play (or scenes). The first time should be a cold reading, so that people can comment on what they thought it was before they actually knew. Since only the introductory reading of the work can be cold, take advantage of that fact.

Cast the roles at the table. Whenever possible, use different actors from act to act, or even scene to scene. That way, the writer hears different voices; even when they are not the ideal ones, there are lessons to be learned from listening to different takes on the same character. In addition, the actors become more collegial and less competitive; there is no reason for them to compete when no one is being cast.

DISCUSSION RULES

Discussion begins with the moderator soliciting comments from those around the table. Only the invited participants of the group should comment; outside observers are asked to simply observe. When someone wishes to speak, they raise their hand or otherwise signal for recognition, but they do not interrupt out of turn, which would lead to outspoken members dominating the comments and more reserved artists rarely being able to share their observations.

The first round of observations consists of comments only. Direct questions should wait until the next stage of discussion. During these initial comments, the writer should not respond to any critique. This will prevent the writer from becoming quickly defensive, and require him or her to listen to what everyone thought the play was and wasn't doing, whether that matched the written intention or not. Such realizations can be quite useful.

After the first wave of comments have been heard, the moderator will summarize and synthesize the major points that keep recurring in people's perspectives, as well as add other observations that have not yet been made. The moderator's remarks will function as a bridge to the next stage, which will be further comments or direct questions. At this point, the writer should feel free to respond to anything at all.

At all times, participants should express agreement or disagreement with any comment by employing a thumbs up or down gesture rather than by repeating or rephrasing the observation. The moderator will take note of thumbs when such displays warrant notice.

Discussion will continue until the writer has had all his or her questions addressed.

During the discussion, there are four rules that shall be observed and will, if necessary, be enforced. They are as follows:

(1) All comments must be constructive. No trashing is allowed, ever. Comments such as "I hate these people, I wish they'd die" help no one. It is far more useful to note that an audience might feel more involved if given more reason to care about these characters and what happens to them.

(2) All comments must address the play being written, not the one you would have written (even if you are convinced yours might have been better). Everyone is there to help the writer write the play *that writer* aspires to write. If the play is about cowboys, it is irrelevant that it does no justice to the Apache. Nor does it matter whether it is radical or revolutionary or reactionary; what matters is whether whatever pattern it is trying to establish requires more yellow in the corner.

(3) No invidious comparisons are allowed. It is unhelpful to say that Shakespeare did this better or that Jane Austen's work has a more mature perspective on the issue. Limit comments to the work at hand.

(4) No one, ever, is allowed to tell a writer how to rewrite. They know how to rewrite, and why they may choose not to. Wonder aloud whether knowing more about a character's motivation might be helpful to this story; do *not* say "what you need is a scene in which Mark enters the room, shoots six people and then drinks some lemonade."

Within these parameters, comments are welcomed.

Introduction

This is the second volume of *Plays from New River*, showcasing a place where gifted writers of plays and screenplays are paid and nurtured to write whatever they most want to write. These three very different plays are among the results. *Feasting on Cardigans* was developed at New River Dramatists and presented by the Oberon Theatre Ensemble at the Midtown International Theatre Festival at the Workshop Theatre in New York City in July 2005. *Tiger in the Tree* is a new play that was written and developed at New River. It explores fundamental mysteries of life in an unusual way, when a strange woman shows up at a writer's house and seems to know absolutely everything about him, while he has no idea who she is or what she wants. And *Baseball Game of the Week* reminds us of our love of tradition and how we relate our sports and games to the essence of our national character.

Mark Eisman's *Feasting on Cardigans* explores with whimsical humor a pair of dedicated exterminators and the emotional effect they have on those their lives touch in uniquely comic fashion. A seriously funny play about love, life, death, birth, and moths, it explores major themes with an offbeat charm that wins over audiences.

Tiger in the Tree is an intriguing thriller that as it proceeds becomes about much more than one might assume at the beginning. When a strange visitor invades his home, an assimilated Latino writer is forced to face truths and consequences about his work and his life that change both of them, forever.

James McLure's *Baseball Game of the Week* is a deceptively moving, always funny meditation on progress, memory and baseball. "Jim McLure's insight, talent, love of language and sheer humanity inspired not only us who loved him but a whole new generation of writers who came to appreciate his gentle tutelage and beguiling insight to their work."—Greg Johnson, artistic director, Montana Repertory Theatre.

Feasting on Cardigans
by Mark Eisman

Feasting on Cardigans was developed at New River Dramatists and presented by the Oberon Theatre Ensemble at the Midtown International Theatre Festival at The Workshop Theatre in New York City in July 2005.

★ ★ ★

Characters
HAAF (27)   LENAH (27)   ROSE-MARIE (27)
DUNCAN (16)   CRESCENT (33)

Place: New York City (Various Locations, Unit Set)
Time: The Near Future

ACT ONE

(An intensely bright spotlight illuminates a section of an otherwise dark stage. A pair of "stage moths" gravitate towards the light. When that light goes out, HAFF and LENAH appear in two pools of light on opposite sides of the stage. During the scene, they move gradually closer to each other. Stage moths hover around their lights.)

HAFF. First time around for both of us.

LENAH. I thought I was serious with a couple of cops. *(LENAH laughs.)*

HAFF. It was hard enough spending a couple of hours with some of the girls I got fixed up with, let alone a life.

LENAH. *(turning to face HAFF)* Haff and I completely agree.

HAFF. Which is a little scary but really cool.

LENAH. Our favorite cereal…

HAFF. Total.

LENAH. With fresh strawberries.

HAFF. And if we can't get strawberries, we won't settle for bananas.

LENAH. We hate summer.

HAFF. We prefer winter.

LENAH. But not as much as fall.

HAFF. We love this city.

LENAH. We will never leave it.

HAFF. We don't like strangers.

LENAH. Or cakes with liquor in them. And one thing we are in absolute agreement about.

HAFF. Not one thing, everything.

LENAH. We don't want children.

HAFF. We don't.

LENAH. What a relief. I want to marry Haff. I want to spend the rest of my life with him but I will not under any circumstances become a mother.

HAFF. *(shooing a stage moth with his hand)* Most people have kids and what happens is either you wreck them or they wreck you unless they turn out great, which can happen, but it's such a responsibility and I for one don't want it. Too risky.

LENAH. I am in total agreement.

HAFF. Just the two of us. That's it.

LENAH. *(brushing moth away)* You've got to be certain, Haff.

HAFF. I am.

LENAH. Because I am never going to change my mind about this. Just the thought of becoming a mother makes me sick.

HAFF. It turns my stomach and I spend my days with vermin.

LENAH. *(needs to brush a moth away before she kisses him)* Who would have thought that the man I love would be an exterminator?

HAFF. We help people and they still think we're creepy.

LENAH. I've only had two other boyfriends and they've both been cops. Of course, I never loved them. Cops are not easy to love.

HAFF. You're easy.

LENAH. I am not.

HAFF. For me you were and nobody's ever been easy for me. Should we tell my mother?

LENAH. Tell her what?

HAFF. That she's never going to be a grandmother.

LENAH. What about your sister?

HAFF. We think Jane's a lesbian. What do you think?

LENAH. I've only met her once. Probably.

HAFF. She hasn't told us anything. Nobody tells anybody anything anymore.

LENAH. Haff, lesbians have children constantly.

HAFF. It amazes me how people just don't realize how children change everything. Sometimes in a good way but a lot of times in not such a good way.

LENAH. You don't have to convince me, but I just want you to understand. I am never going to change my mind about this. Never.

HAFF. Great.

LENAH. Would you leave me if I did?

HAFF. I would never leave you.

LENAH. I would expect you to.

HAFF. You would. Would you leave me?

LENAH. *(snapping her fingers)* Like that!

HAFF. *(snapping his fingers)* Then I would leave you like that.

LENAH. We absolutely feel the same way. (LENAH *embraces him.*)

LENAH. We are so lucky!

HAFF. Uh-huh.

LENAH. *(brushing away moth)* What's with the moths?

HAFF. Turn out the light.

LENAH. They are irritating.

HAFF. The light, Lenah, the light.

(*The light does go out. LIGHTS UP full on the stage, which is ringed by a series of doors.* HAFF *and* ROSE-MARIE *go in and out of the various doors, tossing woolen articles of clothes out as they do.* ROSE-MARIE *holds up a pair of moth eaten pants.*)

ROSE-MARIE. Those moths sure picnicked on these pants.

HAFF. Better moths than rats.

ROSE-MARIE. Hey, I'm not complaining.

HAFF. Better moths than mice even.

ROSE-MARIE. I was just asking, how come all of a sudden moths?

HAFF. Pests have cycles.

ROSE-MARIE. When was the last moth cycle?

HAFF. The summer of '55, according to my grandfather.

ROSE-MARIE. Do you come from a long line of exterminators?

HAFF. My father sold life insurance instead.

ROSE-MARIE. I'm the first in my family. Everybody else is a waitress or a nurse, the women that is. The men tend to be bartenders and mechanics.

HAFF. You're the first female exterminator I've ever met.

ROSE-MARIE. I prefer exterminating to waitressing.

HAFF. Who wouldn't?

ROSE-MARIE. And I'm better at it.

HAFF. You've got a special gift for roaches, Rose-Marie.

ROSE-MARIE. Where have all the roaches gone?

HAFF. Not their cycle.

ROSE-MARIE. Did we kill them all, Haff?

HAFF. Don't be so naïve. They'll be back.

ROSE-MARIE. Because roaches, I know. Roaches, I'm good at. I'm still pretty insecure about moths.

HAFF. We all are.

ROSE-MARIE. It makes me feel better to hear you say that because you really know your stuff. When you kill something, it stays killed.

HAFF. Stop.

ROSE-MARIE. There's nothing that you can't exterminate.

HAFF. Thank you. That's really...

ROSE-MARIE. Of course, it's not enough to kill.

HAFF. That's true.

ROSE-MARIE. You have to make sure a whole new generation of pests doesn't spring up and that's something I've learned how to do from you. You are so excellent at total elimination.

HAFF. Nobody has ever appreciated what I do before.

ROSE-MARIE. I am looking forward to learning about moth control... at your feet.

HAFF. I haven't had a lot of previous moth experience.

ROSE-MARIE. Maybe you could ask your grandfather.

HAFF. He doesn't remember anything anymore. Just that there was a time when this city had clothes moths and it's been fifty years and now all of a sudden they're back.

ROSE-MARIE. We'll get 'em.

HAFF. I share your confidence.

ROSE-MARIE. Moths are weird.

HAFF. What do you mean?

ROSE-MARIE. Rats'll eat practically anything. So will mice and roaches, but these guys only eat wool. Talk about picky!

HAFF. Primarily but not only wool. *(ROSE-MARIE takes out notebook and pencil.)*

HAFF. They may eat fur.

ROSE-MARIE. That I did not know.

HAFF. If they can't get wool. Sometimes, in extreme desperation, feathers.

ROSE-MARIE. So if there's a wool hat with a feather, do they eat the whole thing?

HAFF. They never eat the whole thing. You've seen what they do.

ROSE-MARIE. They just make holes. Then they go on to something else. Sometimes they just make little holes. Big holes, little holes, the garment is still ruined. We'll kill them, Haff, won't we?

HAFF. There isn't any infestation in this city that cannot be controlled.

ROSE-MARIE. I admire optimists.

(HAFF and ROSE-MARIE start circulating through the closets again, tossing out more moth-eaten garments into a pile on the stage. LIGHTS UP on LENAH with her operator headset.)

LENAH. 911... What is your emergency? ... Is he breathing? ... You're not sure... What is your address, please... Yes, ma'am, if he moved, it would be very likely that he is breathing. We'll get an ambulance out to you as soon as possible... 911... What is your emergency? ... When you say you're going out of your mind, could you be more specific, sir?

(LIGHTS DOWN on LENAH. LIGHTS UP on CRESCENT, DUNCAN, HAFF and ROSE-MARIE. CRESCENT holds up wool garments with holes in them.)

CRESCENT. This is all your fault, Duncan.

DUNCAN. It wasn't my moths.

CRESCENT. Then whose moths were they?

DUNCAN. Ask the exterminators. *(to HAFF and ROSE-MARIE)* Tell her.

HAFF. They weren't your son's moths, ma'am.

CRESCENT. But he collects these things. And he's not my son.

DUNCAN. My collection is dead.

CRESCENT. Look at this cardigan, ruined.

DUNCAN. Dead things don't eat sweaters, auntie.

HAFF. Your nephew is correct, ma'am.

CRESCENT. He had some live ones.

DUNCAN. I had a butterfly when I was thirteen years old.

CRESCENT. A butterfly is not a normal pet for a teenage boy.

ROSE-MARIE. Butterflies, living or dead, don't eat cardigans either, ma'am.

DUNCAN. I don't have the butterfly anymore. I freed it and then was filled with regret.

CRESCENT. It probably laid eggs or pupas or whatever butterflies lay all over this apartment.

DUNCAN. Your ignorance about pupas is glaring. *(DUNCAN exits into closet)*

CRESCENT. He's not really mine.

HAFF. We can treat your infestation, but you'll have to be patient.

CRESCENT. He's my nephew. I agreed to raise him.

ROSE-MARIE. How many closets in total do you have?

CRESCENT. Just this one and Duncan's and the other one.

HAFF. Any infestation in the other one?

CRESCENT. It's mainly for storage. My brother's things.

(CRESCENT opens a closet. HAFF and ROSE-MARIE bring out several suits and other clothing, all of which are badly moth eaten with huge holes in them.)

CRESCENT. Oh my God! Ruined! My brother will have nothing to wear when he gets home.

HAFF. When do you expect him?

DUNCAN. *(emerging from his closet)* In ten to fifteen years, if he's lucky.

ROSE-MARIE. Where is he?

DUNCAN & CRESCENT. Attica.

ROSE-MARIE. Oh.

DUNCAN. My dad shot my mom. That's why I'm living with my aunt.

CRESCENT. There were extenuating circumstances.

DUNCAN. He caught her allegedly screwing the electrician.

CRESCENT. This was such a nice blue suit.

ROSE-MARIE. Don't they give convicts new suits when they get out?

HAFF. I think they only give new suits in old movies.

CRESCENT. And nothing as nice as this… was.

DUNCAN. He may never get out.

CRESCENT. Let's be optimistic, Duncan.

DUNCAN. That's what I was being. I hope he never gets out.

HAFF. Why do you say that?

CRESCENT. No need to tell the pest control people everything, Duncan.

DUNCAN. My father is a son of a bitch and I hope he dies behind bars. *(DUNCAN exits behind closet door, slamming it.)*

CRESCENT. Duncan is still a little bitter. You have kids?

ROSE-MARIE. No ma'am.

HAFF. My fiancée and I have decided not to have any children.

CRESCENT. Very wise.

ROSE-MARIE. You mean not right away?

HAFF. I mean… not ever.

ROSE-MARIE. When did you get engaged?

HAFF. Late last night.

ROSE-MARIE. Congratulations.

CRESCENT. I wanted to be a mother so badly and it just didn't seem to be in the cards for me. Then Barry shot Sally and I got Duncan. I thought it was a wonderful miracle at first.

HAFF. Shouldn't you keep your voice down?

CRESCENT. He never listens to me.

ROSE-MARIE. What's the point of even getting married if you don't want children?

HAFF. Because you love each other. Marriage is about love. It isn't about children.

CRESCENT. Do I need mothballs or what?

HAFF. It's not as simple as balls anymore.

CRESCENT. My red pajamas. Where are my red pajamas? I wonder if they've gotten to them. I only wear them once or twice a year but I do adore my red pajamas. They're flannel, fire engine red flannel. Is flannel wool?

HAFF. Generally. Unless your red pajamas are a cotton blend.

CRESCENT. Do they eat blends?

HAFF. If they're desperate.

ROSE-MARIE. They often are,

(CRESCENT *runs into a closet door. Her moan is heard. LIGHTS DOWN. LIGHTS UP on* LENAH *taking her coat off and hanging it in another closet. She turns around to face* HAFF, *who embraces her. Controlled at work,* LENAH *tends to be on the verge of hysteria at home.*)

(HAFF *takes* LENAH's *coat from closet, examines it for holes.*)

LENAH. What?

HAFF. *(returning coat to closet)* Nothing.

LENAH. Please don't do that.

HAFF. What?

LENAH. Tell me it's nothing when it's obviously something.

HAFF. Sorry. I think we may be in for an epidemic.

LENAH. Epidemic!

HAFF. I didn't mean to alarm you.

LENAH. Epidemic is a very alarming word, Haff.

HAFF. For the first time since the mid 1950s, the city's closets are being widely infiltrated by clothes moths.

LENAH. An epidemic is when something contagious spreads and people die.

HAFF. Nobody's dying. Nobody's going to die. Just a lot of coats and sweaters and scarves and old hats with feathers. Something happen at work? You seem a little jittery.

LENAH. Something always happens at work. I'm a 911 dispatcher.

HAFF. What happened today?

LENAH. I think this woman was being killed.

HAFF. Don't you get a lot of that?

LENAH. Actually, this was my first possible murder in progress.

HAFF. Why do you say possible?

LENAH. She was screaming "He's going to kill me! He's going to kill me!" That might have been an exaggeration.

HAFF. Did it sound like he was killing her?

LENAH. No. It sounded like she was alone. I didn't hear anyone else at all.

HAFF. Can't you kill someone without making any noise?

LENAH. I have no idea. She didn't say he's killing me, she said he's going to kill me. I remained calm and in control.

HAFF. That sounds kind of vague. Was she drunk?

LENAH. She was hysterical.

HAFF. Was she also drunk?

LENAH. I've talked to enough drunks with phony emergencies. She didn't sound intoxicated.

HAFF. So you sent the cops.

LENAH. Of course I did!

HAFF. So can't you find out what happened?

LENAH. We're not supposed to do that.

HAFF. Oh.

LENAH. Unless we screwed up. Then they let us know.

HAFF. You ever screw up?

LENAH. Once.

HAFF. Once is not very much. What happened?

LENAH. Heard an address wrong.

HAFF. And...

LENAH. An ambulance was late.

HAFF. I could use a drink. Could you?

LENAH. Yes. That would be good.

HAFF. You want to go out?

LENAH. No.

HAFF. Is there anything to drink?

LENAH. Only diet Doctor P.

HAFF. When we're married...

LENAH. Yes.

HAFF. Let's always have a little booze around the place.

LENAH. We're not big drinkers.

HAFF. That's why I said a little booze.

LENAH. God, I really do love you.

HAFF. Yes.

LENAH. So are we infested?

HAFF. Not at the moment.

LENAH. I feel much better... safer... better.

(They kiss.)

NEWSCASTER'S VOICE. The Pest Control Department has set up a special hotline to deal with moths only. Do not call the ratline or the mouseline. Call the new mothline.

(LIGHTS UP on HAFF and ROSE-MARIE. Each carries a large black trash bag.)

ROSE-MARIE. Am I crazy or are moths harder than mice?

HAFF. You think you're crazy? I'm having these dreams about this moth couple.

ROSE-MARIE. What happens in the dream?

HAFF. All I remember is that she's very... controlling.

(They dump cereal boxes from their trash bags out.)

ROSE-MARIE. And now we're starting to get them in Rice Krispies.

HAFF. Grain moths. Different bug. Different treatment.

ROSE-MARIE. *(taking out a Cocoa Puffs box)* I've seen my share of vermin damage but those infested Cocoa Puffs...

HAFF. Gross.

ROSE-MARIE. That little girl is going to need extensive counseling.

HAFF. Send a kid for professional help just because she found a few bugs in her cereal. That would only make things worse. I would never do that. Now that's crazy.

ROSE-MARIE. Thought you weren't going to have any kids.

HAFF. We're not.

ROSE-MARIE. You were real good with that child. Got her to stop screaming... for a while.

HAFF. So what? They're more trouble than they're worth.

ROSE-MARIE. Can't say that till you're a father, Haff.

HAFF. This is still a free country. I can say anything I want. And who are you to talk? You don't have any.

ROSE-MARIE. I had one.

HAFF. What do you mean had?

ROSE-MARIE. For a couple of guys.

HAFF. Huh?

ROSE-MARIE. My friends, Stu and Alan.

HAFF. Oh I get you. You see it?

ROSE-MARIE. It's a girl. Her name is Sandy. I'm her Aunt Rose-Marie.

HAFF. Aunt? You're her mother.

ROSE-MARIE. I'm more like an aunt.

HAFF. Well as long as there's no responsibility, you're O.K.

ROSE-MARIE. I baby sit.

HAFF. How old is she?

ROSE-MARIE. Four. Want to see her picture?

HAFF. I got to get home. I'll never forget that child pointing at her cereal in terror and all that spilled milk.

ROSE-MARIE. Are there certain cereals they won't eat?

HAFF. Kids?

ROSE-MARIE. Grain moths. If clothes moths only eat wool, maybe grain moths...

HAFF. *(picking up box of Total)* No not Total too. That's what Lenah and I love.

ROSE-MARIE. I'm sure your personal Totals are uninfested.

HAFF. How can anybody be sure of anything anymore?

ROSE-MARIE. *(shaking Kix box)* We must root them out of every box of Kix in the city.

HAFF. Kix! You really are a devoted exterminator, Rose-Marie.

ROSE-MARIE. Extermination is my life.

(ROSE-MARIE opens a box of Wheaties, indicates something disturbing inside. LIGHTS DOWN on HAFF and ROSE-MARIE. LIGHTS UP on LENAH.)

LENAH. 911. What is your emergency? ... That is not an emergency, sir... I do understand how you feel, but a lost dog is not an emergency... put up posters, sir! This line is only for legitimate emergencies. I don't have time to give you an example... Yes, sir, you have to be practically dying. That's a very useful guideline.

(LIGHTS DOWN on LENAH. LIGHTS UP on HAFF, CRESCENT and DUNCAN.)

CRESCENT. Thank you for coming.

HAFF. I was under the impression that your infestation was under control.

CRESCENT. It is, but I thought you could talk to Duncan. *(whispering)* You'll be paid for your time.

HAFF. I don't talk, ma'am. I spray.

CRESCENT. He seems to be laboring under a misconception that only you can straighten out. I'm sorry what's your first name again?

HAFF. Haff.

DUNCAN. As in wit.

HAFF. Haven't heard that since I was in the tenth grade.

DUNCAN. That's what I'm in.

HAFF. O.K. You're entitled.

DUNCAN. I mean, is that really your name?

HAFF. Two F's, no L. Short for Hafford.

DUNCAN. Weird!

CRESCENT. I'll be in the kitchen so you guys can talk.

(CRESCENT *exits through one of the doors ringing the stage.*)

HAFF. Your aunt said you wanted to talk to me about something.

DUNCAN. I don't even know you. Why would I want to talk to you?

HAFF. Hey, I'm very busy right now.

DUNCAN. I know and it's all my fault.

HAFF. How's that?

DUNCAN. I'm into moths.

HAFF. I remember.

DUNCAN. Heavily into moths.

HAFF. Uh-huh.

DUNCAN. I'm the only person I know who's heavily into moths.

HAFF. You know me.

DUNCAN. No, I don't.

HAFF. I'm heavily into bugs.

DUNCAN. Killing 'em.

HAFF. The bad ones.

DUNCAN. That's the thing. I don't think of them as bad. I really don't. They're just living their lives.

HAFF. I understand.

DUNCAN. Nobody understands. It's just Kill! Kill! Kill!

HAFF. They called me Bugs.

(DUNCAN *laughs.*)

HAFF. That what they call you too?

DUNCAN. They call me the Donut… 'cause my first name's Duncan. Get it? Sometimes they call me the Hole. I prefer the Donut to the Hole.

HAFF. I had a pretty good collection.

DUNCAN. Moths?

HAFF. All kinds of insects.

DUNCAN. I'm never been interested in anything but moths and to a much lesser extent, butterflies. Andrea Flewelling started this rumor.

HAFF. What's her nickname?

DUNCAN. She doesn't have one. She's popular. That I was responsible for everybody's coats and sweaters being eaten.

HAFF. Why would she say something like that?

DUNCAN. Because she's an idiot, only she's gorgeous so she's not.

HAFF. Or nobody says she is... yet. One day she'll wake up and find that she's nothing but a dumb old broad.

DUNCAN. Right. Right. So anyhow she kept saying that I started this whole thing and I kept saying that was insane and then in the cafeteria, I took responsibility for it.

HAFF. Why would you do that?

DUNCAN. I don't know. I thought it would be cool. That it would make me look powerful.

HAFF. That is... weird.

DUNCAN. I am weird. I dream about moths mating all the time. I think that's what they're doing. Is that what they're doing? Is that why there are so many of them?

HAFF. This is just part of a cycle. The current infestation has nothing to do with you or your dreams.

DUNCAN. Then why were we infested before any of our neighbors?

HAFF. Duncan, I treated an apartment filled with ravaged tweeds twenty blocks away a full two weeks before I ever entered your closet.

DUNCAN. Not my closet. My closet was O.K. I only wear artificial fabrics. My father's closet. They made really big holes in all of his things, totally destroyed his sweaters. They only ate my aunt's pajamas.

HAFF. Your aunt is primarily acrylic.

DUNCAN. And they don't touch any manmade fibers.

HAFF. That's right.

DUNCAN. They'd sooner starve to death than eat anything unnatural.

HAFF. Moths don't think about death, Duncan.

DUNCAN. How do you know?

HAFF. Some moths are attracted to light, some to wool, some to grains. The wool eating moths shun the light. The moths who gravitate to the light have no interest in fabrics or breakfast cereals. You can't lump all moths together.

DUNCAN. I've made some new friends since I've taken responsibility for the infestation. They're a little strange but I don't get the impression that any of them is going to shoot the cheerleaders or anything.

HAFF. Did you tell your… your father about all of this?

DUNCAN. I don't tell him anything. I don't see him.

HAFF. Why's that?

DUNCAN. He killed my mom.

HAFF. How old were you?

DUNCAN. Nine months. I slept through it. How can you sleep through your father shooting your mother?

HAFF. Babies do that.

DUNCAN. Do you have any children?

HAFF. No. My fiancée and I aren't going to have any.

DUNCAN. What, are you sterile or something? Sorry.

HAFF. No, I am not! We just don't want any.

DUNCAN. That is so smart. I am a living example of how bad children turn out.

HAFF. You're not bad, Duncan.

DUNCAN. That's what my therapist keeps saying. What else is she going to say?

HAFF. Hey, what kid wouldn't be fucked up if his father shot his mother?

DUNCAN. My therapist says that too only without the "f" word.

HAFF. Sorry. I didn't mean to…

DUNCAN. That's O.K., Haff. I like the "f" word, when it's used sparingly and passionately and I have the feeling that's the way you use it. Sometimes, when I have those dreams about moths effing, they occasionally metamorphosize into people effing. I never told anybody that.

(HAFF looks at his watch.)

DUNCAN. Sorry to have taken up so much of your important time.

HAFF. No, that's O.K.

DUNCAN. When will you be back?

HAFF. Second Saturday of every month, kid.

DUNCAN. What if…

HAFF. What?

DUNCAN. Nothing. Never mind.

(LIGHTS DOWN. There is a scream in the dark. LIGHTS UP on LENAH holding a sweater with holes in it. HAFF emerges from another closet door.)

LENAH. *(holding the sweater up to him)* You told me you had taken precautions.

HAFF. I had.

LENAH. Then how does something like this happen?

HAFF. That's an old sweater.

LENAH. So?

HAFF. Sometimes old sweaters just get holes in 'em, honey.

LENAH. Are you saying this is my fault?

HAFF. I'm not saying it's anyone's fault, Leanie.

LENAH. You're saying these things just happen.

HAFF. Yes.

LENAH. Well, I'm saying it was them. Them!

HAFF. O.K. it was them.

LENAH. Please don't do that.

HAFF. Do what?

LENAH. Say you agree with me when you obviously don't. We agreed that we weren't going to humor each other.

HAFF. Let me look at that sweater.

(LENAH *hands* HAFF *the sweater. He examines the holes more closely.*)

HAFF. What else you got in that closet?

LENAH. Everything is in that closet.

HAFF. You need to check your other garments.

LENAH. I don't want them crawling all over me.

HAFF. They don't do that. Don't be a baby.

LENAH. We can both fit. Come into the closet with me.

(LENAH *holds out her hand to* HAFF. *They disappear into a closet. After a few seconds, another sweater is tossed out of the closet, followed by a scarf, followed by a coat, followed by another scarf, followed by a robe and a hat, followed by* HAFF *and* LENAH.)

LENAH. Do you still think it's something other than them?

HAFF. No. It's them all right. Them!

LENAH. *(examining devastated scarves)* They really do a job on scarves.

HAFF. It does seem to be their favorite food.

LENAH. My beautiful black suit!

(LENAH *dashes back into the closet.* HAFF *remains on the outside, examining the other garments. From the closet,* LENAH *shrieks.*)

HAFF. Honey, are you all right in there? I'm coming in!

(HAFF *rejoins* LENAH *in the closet.*)

LENAH. *(off)* Look.

HAFF. *(off)* I'm sorry I don't see anything.

LENAH. *(off)* Then feel.

LENAH. *(off)* Don't feel anything either. I'm sorry.

(HAFF and LENAH emerge from the closet with LENAH's black suit.)

LENAH. Right there.

HAFF. I don't even know that I'd call that a hole.

LENAH. Whatever you call it, it's in my ass. It's in the ass part of my black suit. You expect me to go to a funeral with a hole in my ass.

HAFF. Maybe you can mend it.

LENAH. I don't sew.

HAFF. You don't?

LENAH. Are you disappointed? You want to call off the wedding?

HAFF. We need to talk about that… the wedding.

LENAH. Please don't change the subject.

HAFF. You were the one who brought it up… the wedding.

LENAH. I would not like to be married in something with holes.

HAFF. Never saw a bride in black wool. And incidentally, I do sew.

LENAH. Really?

HAFF. A little. Want me to see if I can fix the hole in your ass?

LENAH. Even I know that moth holes are unsewable. Just get rid of the damn things.

HAFF. I'm doing my best. Every day I go out there and I do battle with them!

LENAH. *(touching his face)* You're a very devoted exterminator, my love, but they're winning.

(LENAH puts her arms around him.)

HAFF. I feel lousy about your clothes.

LENAH. You didn't personally eat them.

HAFF. But I do feel personally responsible.

LENAH. And I do expect you to personally kill them.

HAFF. We do not kill, Lenah. We exterminate.

(*HAFF and ROSE-MARIE weave in and out of the various closets. The sound of exterminating devices are heard. They finally emerge from the same closet.*)

HAFF. (*looking at tag on ROSE-MARIE's sweater*) Acrylic.

ROSE-MARIE. It's not because I'm afraid of wool.

HAFF. They won't touch acrylic or any other manmade fiber. At least, that has always been our belief. Let's just hope there isn't a new breed of less discriminating moths.

ROSE-MARIE. The kind that would settle for polyester.

HAFF. That's scary.

ROSE-MARIE. Who knows how a moth's mind works?

HAFF. They don't exactly have minds.

ROSE-MARIE. I know that. I was just speaking metaphorically.

HAFF. What?

ROSE-MARIE. I was an English major at City University. I never graduated.

HAFF. How come?

ROSE-MARIE. I got a summer job as an exterminator's assistant.

HAFF. And that was it for you?

ROSE-MARIE. Why go back to college when you find out what you want to do for the rest of your life and it sure as hell isn't English? I presume you feel the same way I do?

HAFF. It was a family business.

ROSE-MARIE. I thought you said it skipped a generation.

HAFF. Yes. My father wanted to do something else. He didn't have the stomach for vermin. Would you encourage your daughter to go into pest control?

ROSE-MARIE. She's not my daughter. I just gave birth to her.

HAFF. I'm sorry. I didn't know what to call her.

ROSE-MARIE. That's all right. I don't think it's genetic.

HAFF. What?

ROSE-MARIE. A talent for extermination. I don't think it's inherited like a beautiful voice or a head for physics or green eyes or fat ankles. And you can't really judge from whether she swats flies or crushes ants. I hardly ever see Sandy.

HAFF. Your... this child.

ROSE-MARIE. I want to have another one.

HAFF. That you keep.

ROSE-MARIE. Yes. I want to be a single mother.

HAFF. Maybe you'll meet somebody that you like.

ROSE-MARIE. I've already given up on all that. I stopped dating permanently when I became a full time exterminator. It was either men or mice.

(ROSE-MARIE *laughs at her little joke.*)

HAFF. You shouldn't give up. I never thought I'd fall in love either and then I did.

ROSE-MARIE. You got to be lucky to fall in love.

HAFF. I guess you could say that. So are you going to get the gay guys to fertilize you?

ROSE-MARIE. I doubt it. *(fixing gaze on HAFF)* I'm still looking for the right person.

HAFF. Maybe just some stranger would be best.

ROSE-MARIE. I don't think so.

HAFF. Maybe some very handsome genius or something.

ROSE-MARIE. I don't want things that everybody else wants.

HAFF. Neither do I.

(ROSE-MARIE *puts the sweater back on. They start circulating through the closets again.*)

CRESCENT. I just wanted to thank you for all you've done.

HAFF. You don't want to let down your guard. Replenish your moth crystals on a regular basis. Be safe. Wear cotton.

CRESCENT. I was speaking of your work with my nephew.

HAFF. I just talked to the kid.

CRESCENT. And that's an achievement in itself. I try and fail. Boys need to have a male role model.

HAFF. I'm hardly a... model.

CRESCENT. You understand the boy better than I ever will. I just don't want Duncan to follow in his father's footsteps.

HAFF. I don't think Duncan will murder his wife.

CRESCENT. That's reassuring. Of course, he probably won't marry at all. He's a true loner and true loners never marry.

HAFF. I was kind of a loner myself and I'm engaged.

CRESCENT. That's right. Who's the lucky girl?

HAFF. Her name's Lenah. She's a 911 operator.

CRESCENT. That sounds like a very stressful job for a woman... or anybody. So when's the wedding?

HAFF. We need to talk about that. We're not in any hurry.

CRESCENT. She's obviously not... well, you said you weren't going to be having any little Haffs.

HAFF. We are in complete agreement about that.

CRESCENT. I can understand how you feel.

HAFF. Most people don't.

CRESCENT. They can be a blessing but what few people are willing to admit is they can also be an unbearable lifelong guilt-drenching curse.

HAFF. Is that how you feel about Duncan?

CRESCENT. If he were my son, I might consider him a curse. Since he's only my nephew, he's more of a burden. Forgive my frankness.

HAFF. I think honesty is a very important quality.

CRESCENT. In a woman?

HAFF. In anyone.

CRESCENT. More peach pie?

HAFF. No, thank you. It's very good.

CRESCENT. It's not mine.

HAFF. Didn't think it was.

CRESCENT. It isn't even Sara Lee's.

(DUNCAN enters, home from school.)

DUNCAN. Hi, Haff. Are they back?

HAFF. Just my monthly visit.

DUNCAN. You've never come on a school day before.

CRESCENT. *(exiting into closet)* I'll just muse on side dishes for dinner and make myself scarce.

HAFF. So how's it going, Duncan?

DUNCAN. Some hockey players tried to make me eat a roach.

HAFF. Living or dead?

DUNCAN. In a jar. Not sure.

HAFF. So, you didn't eat it?

DUNCAN. No. They ran away when they saw the guidance counselor coming.

HAFF. Anybody who's scared of a guidance counselor isn't much of a man.

DUNCAN. Anybody ever make you eat anything?

HAFF. My mom made me eat liver.

DUNCAN. My aunt is a terrible cook except for breakfast food but she never makes me eat anything. Have you ever mated moths?

HAFF. When I was a kid.

DUNCAN. My age?

HAFF. Younger than you.

DUNCAN. Was it fun?

HAFF. A blast!

DUNCAN. It's something I want to do. I've been thinking about it and thinking about it.

HAFF. Maybe this isn't the best time.

DUNCAN. Of year?

HAFF. I mean... with moths making the news.

DUNCAN. I saw that! On PBS even. I wouldn't be mating clothes moths.

HAFF. People tend to lump moths, the way they tend to lump people.

DUNCAN. Can you tell me how to mate?

HAFF. You don't know.

DUNCAN. I have a vague idea.

HAFF. What kind of moth do you want to mate?

DUNCAN. A Polyphemus.

HAFF. They're real easy to mate.

DUNCAN. I'm not totally ignorant. Most male moths only live a week. Their only purpose is to find a mate and make sexual contact with her. Then she lays her eggs. Then they die. Is that accurate?

HAFF. For the most part.

DUNCAN. Is it true that the male and female may possibly remain coupled for up to twenty four hours?

HAFF. That seems like a very long time. The way I did it was to put the female's cage out at night.

DUNCAN. She gives off some sort of powerful sexual scent that attracts the male.

HAFF. Right.

DUNCAN. I don't think that works in the city. There are too many other competing odors.

HAFF. I did it in the city.

DUNCAN. And it worked?

HAFF. Ahuh.

DUNCAN. That was a long time ago. How many babies did you have?

HAFF. Quite a few.

DUNCAN. Did you raise them?

HAFF. I wouldn't exactly...

DUNCAN. You didn't raise the baby caterpillars and have them spin their own cocoons?

HAFF. Oh sure, I did that.

DUNCAN. That sounds like the best part.

HAFF. It was.

DUNCAN. So you'll help me?

HAFF. If you have any more questions, I'll be glad to answer them but it seems to me you have pretty good instructions there. *(looking at watch)* Oh my gosh, I don't know what happens when I start talking with you...

DUNCAN. Thanks, Haff. I appreciate the time you give me. I do.

HAFF. You are so much like I was... It's a little scary.

DUNCAN. So it does get better?

HAFF. Contrary to what people say, these are not the happiest years of your life.

DUNCAN. If they were, I'd probably kill myself!

(LIGHTS DOWN. LIGHTS UP on a frayed looking LENAH. HAFF enters through one of the doors.)

HAFF. Hi.

(LENAH *does not respond.*)

HAFF. Not a good day?

LENAH. You could say that.

HAFF. You want to talk about it or anything?

(LENAH *does not respond.*)

HAFF. Sometimes you do and sometimes you don't.

LENAH. What is wrong with people? Talk about that.

HAFF. Could you be a little more specific?

LENAH. Why are people so stupid?

HAFF. Could you be even more specific?

LENAH. Not at the moment.

(HAFF *starts to exit.*)

LENAH. Where are you going?

HAFF. Just out.

LENAH. You just came in.

HAFF. You look like you want to be alone.

LENAH. *(going up to him)* Look closer.

HAFF. I'm here for you.

LENAH. Is it that people don't understand the meaning of the word? It's not a hard word.

HAFF. Which word is that, Leanie?

LENAH. Emergency!

HAFF. Oh you had one of those days. You want a massage or something?

(HAFF *starts to massage her but she moves away from him.*)

LENAH. A lost dog is not an emergency. Would you agree?

HAFF. I would and you know how I feel about dogs.

LENAH. Your spouse spitting in your face is not an emergency.

HAFF. Somebody actually called 911 because somebody spat at them?

LENAH. A doctor's appointment is not an emergency.

HAFF. Wouldn't that depend on...

LENAH. If you are having a coronary, you do not make an appointment.

HAFF. Absolutely.

LENAH. Define emergency.

HAFF. Danger.

LENAH. What kind of danger?

HAFF. I forget the word.

LENAH. Imminent.

HAFF. That's the word.

LENAH. What if you were raped?

HAFF. If I was going to be raped...

LENAH. If you had been raped, is that an emergency?

HAFF. No.

LENAH. Why not?

HAFF. Because I wasn't in imminent danger. It had already happened.

LENAH. People are so stupid. People are too lazy to look up the number of their local precinct or whatever and all they remember is 911 911 911. So they call it as if we could solve all their foolish little non life-threatening situations.

HAFF. Maybe you should consider transferring to directory assistance.

LENAH. Why would I want to...

HAFF. You just seem kind of stressed.

LENAH. Rather be stressed than bored. Rather save somebody's life than find the number for Radio City Music Hall. You think of me as an operator. I am not. I am a dispatcher.

ACT ONE

HAFF. So, what are you complaining about?

LENAH. What gave you the impression that I was complaining. I was discussing stupid people.

HAFF. People get scared. They panic.

LENAH. We're not like that.

HAFF. No, we're not.

LENAH. An old woman said her hair was on fire. I believed her.

HAFF. Oh my God.

LENAH. I think I helped her. I want to believe I got help to her but you never know. Our volume of calls has gone way up in the last few months.

HAFF. I wonder what that's all about.

LENAH. It has something to do with your arena.

HAFF. People call 911 because of moths?

LENAH. Within the last few months, the volume of pest "emergencies" has ballooned.

HAFF. Wow. Rose-Marie and I were right. They are driving people nuts.

LENAH. A young woman actually said to me : A monster in my closet has eaten my new white sweater.

HAFF. I'm sure it was a little girl.

LENAH. It was a grown woman. I know what children sound like.

HAFF. You get a lot of them?

LENAH. Sometimes... I get mommy isn't moving.

HAFF. Bet you're good with them.

LENAH. I am.... I have been trained to be good with everyone, including every psychopathic moron in this city. We're not supposed to be sympathetic. Sympathy is too intimate for a dispatcher. I aim for crispness.

HAFF. Crispness. Sounds like a good quality if you're a potato chip.

LENAH. Maybe if a rat was chewing your face off.

HAFF. What?

LENAH. That would be an emergency.

HAFF. Rats don't do that.

LENAH. How do you know?

HAFF. Because it happens to be my job and I too am very good...

LENAH. And so you're an expert on what every individual rat does.

HAFF. I've never heard of a rat chewing anybody's face off.

LENAH. What about a hole-making monster?

HAFF. People are used to roaches. Roaches are a part of their lives. They are not used to clothes moths.

LENAH. Just because something is unfamiliar does not make it an emergency.

HAFF. You're right. Lenah, we agree about practically everything.

LENAH. Yes. That's right. I must remember that.

HAFF. So there should be no reason for us to have fights.

LENAH. We can have fights. There should be no reason for us to have disagreements.

(Pause.)

HAFF. I love you.

LENAH. Did you say that because you couldn't come up with anything else to say?

HAFF. You... you... you really know me.

LENAH. And I do love you.

HAFF. And you didn't say that because you couldn't come up with anything else to say.

LENAH. No, but I am stalling and that's something I know better than to do. Time is everything at 911. Time can be life.

HAFF. Are you breaking up with me?

ACT ONE

LENAH. I've just told you that I loved you.

HAFF. It could be: I love you but…

LENAH. I would never do I love you but. You know me better than that.

HAFF. Yes I do, but…

LENAH. Holes.

HAFF. You still getting 'em personally? Jesus Christ, damn those moths!

LENAH. Maybe it's wrong to wholly blame it on a hole. It wasn't like it was the only thing we were using. All the controls in the world apparently weren't enough to protect me.

HAFF. What are you talking about?

LENAH. You can never be safe unless you take drastic invasive measures and that's what I should have done. I was wrong to trust in anything else. Can't blame it on the moths. They don't eat rubber, do they?

HAFF. Never. They'd sooner starve!

LENAH. Then again they're not actually rubber, are they? Do they even call them that anymore? No, everybody says condoms. And they're right out there on display. A man no longer has to ask.

HAFF. Uh-oh.

LENAH. Yes. In the days when rubbers were rubbers, this was called an accident.

HAFF. Did you just find out?

LENAH. Like I said, it was not a good day.

HAFF. We should talk.

LENAH. We already have.

HAFF. We never talked about accidents.

LENAH. What difference does it make? We are in agreement about this. We still are in agreement, aren't we, Haff? That's the beautiful thing about us.

(Pause.)

LENAH. We are, aren't we? Aren't we? Aren't we?

(LENAH's voice trails off as the lights fade around HAFF until he is isolated in a blindingly bright spotlight. LENAH is no longer visible. When her voice is heard, it is the voice of an anonymous operator.)

LENAH. (off) 911... 911... 911... 911.

(HAFF seems drawn to a particular closet door, one that has not been opened, as a moth is drawn to the light. He opens the door. A giant stage moth reminiscent of the movie monster Mothra, made of condomesque material, pops out of the closet. HAFF screams. LENAH's voice repeating "911" continues. The blinding light goes out. End of Act One.)

Act Two

(HAFF's scream continues. LENAH shakes him. LIGHTS UP on HAFF and LENAH in bed.)

HAFF. What?

LENAH. You were screaming.

HAFF. I don't scream.

LENAH. Maybe you were having a nightmare.

HAFF. Maybe you were having a nightmare that I was having a nightmare.

LENAH. It must have been about something truly terrifying.

HAFF. Like what could be so terrifying that it would make me scream out loud?

LENAH. Parenthood.

(They both laugh. HAFF embraces LENAH.)

LENAH. At least, we can still laugh at the same things.

HAFF. Then it's gonna be all right.

LENAH. We're terrible.

HAFF. Are we?

LENAH. No! Accidents happen. We should just be grateful that we have decided by mutual agreement not to make the accident worse. We're putting the accident out of its misery and ours.

(Uncomfortable pause.)

HAFF. Did you?...

LENAH. Did I what?

HAFF. Did you actually go to the doctor or did you just use one of those drugstore things?

LENAH. I used three of those drugstore things.

HAFF. And...

LENAH. Three pinks.

HAFF. Does that mean it's a girl?

LENAH. No.

HAFF. Pink's a boy?

LENAH. Pink just means all the controls in the world screwed up.

HAFF. Should you go to a doctor?

LENAH. I'm going to a clinic.

HAFF. And you wanted to wait for the results of the third test before you said anything to me.

LENAH. I'll take care of this.

HAFF. Should I come?

LENAH. No. I don't need you to. It's a choice, one that we made.

HAFF. Well, not exactly.

LENAH. What do you mean?

HAFF. You're right. I'm just surprised. It wasn't like we were just using condoms.

LENAH. Abstinence is the only fool proof method.

HAFF. It's not a method I would choose.

LENAH. Didn't think so. I need to get my tubes tied. I should have done that a long time ago. You should get yourself fixed too.

HAFF. What are we a couple of dogs? I wondered if you might just put the baby up for adoption.

(Uncomfortable pause.)

LENAH. What baby?

HAFF. If you decide to have it.

LENAH. If we don't want children...

HAFF. We don't.

LENAH. Then why would I want to have something growing in me for nine months and then give it away?

HAFF. I couldn't say.

LENAH. Would you want to have something growing inside of you for nine months and then give it away?

HAFF. I don't have that... choice.

LENAH. No, you do not.

HAFF. I'm sorry I said anything.

LENAH. Why should you be sorry?

HAFF. You seem to be angry again.

LENAH. I never stopped. I just faked it.

HAFF. Mothra.

LENAH. What?

HAFF. I remember my dream. Mothra. It was destroying Tokyo with its latex wings and I got a call to exterminate it.

LENAH. And what did you do?

HAFF. I felt totally... impotent and I woke up screaming.

(LIGHTS DOWN. One patch of light comes up. Stage moth flutters into it.)

NEWSCASTER'S VOICE. A spokeswoman for the division of pest control said that clothes moths have now invaded the darkened closets of Queens, making this a city-wide infestation of epic proportions. "I'm afraid to look at a sweater, let alone put one on my body," said Tracy King, an account executive from Manhattan.

(LIGHTS UP on HAFF and ROSE-MARIE with mothballs in their hands.)

HAFF. They are ineffective.

ROSE-MARIE. They stink.

HAFF. Not like they used to. For years, they sat on drugstore shelves. Now people are hoarding mothballs. And unfortunately, they don't work anymore.

ROSE-MARIE. I wish you and I could come up with a better mothball.

HAFF. Not our job, Rose-Marie.

ROSE-MARIE. If I ever went back to school…

HAFF. You thinking about it?

ROSE-MARIE. If I ever did, maybe I'd learn enough to invent a better mothball.

HAFF. I thought you were an English major.

ROSE-MARIE. I'd switch to what… chemistry, I guess.

HAFF. Yeah… chemistry.

ROSE-MARIE. You think I could learn enough chemistry to invent something?

HAFF. You're smart, Rose-Marie.

ROSE-MARIE. Inventing is probably something that either comes naturally to you or it doesn't.

HAFF. Like exterminating a rat infested public housing complex.

ROSE-MARIE. Yes!

HAFF. Like… having something inside of you growing.

ROSE-MARIE. Yes.

HAFF. That's something that most men will never experience.

ROSE-MARIE. That's true.

HAFF. I meant all men.

ROSE-MARIE. I know you meant that.

HAFF. Although some day… who knows?

ROSE-MARIE. Huh?

HAFF. Maybe in the next millennium or something.

ROSE-MARIE. What?

HAFF. Men will be able to experience the miracle of something growing inside of them. A new life, not a polyp. Anything is possible.

ROSE-MARIE. Except that. That is the one thing that is never going to happen.

HAFF. So you still thinking about becoming an actual mom?

ROSE-MARIE. Yes.

HAFF. Find any candidates yet?

ROSE-MARIE. My first choice would be you.

HAFF. I don't know what to say.

ROSE-MARIE. Don't say anything. I shouldn't have said that.

HAFF. I don't mind that you did.

ROSE-MARIE. I know you don't want any children.

HAFF. This would not be mine.

ROSE-MARIE. It absolutely would not be anyone else's but mine. The father would only make the initial contribution and that would be all.

HAFF. It's something to consider.

ROSE-MARIE. It's just that you have certain genetic qualities that hopefully would transfer to my child.

HAFF. Could I think this over? Are you making a… a… proposition.

ROSE-MARIE. I was just suggesting a possible possibility.

Act Two

HAFF. I don't know if I should tell Lenah. Would you?

ROSE-MARIE. I don't even know her.

HAFF. You must meet each other. I meant, would you tell her if you were me?

ROSE-MARIE. No.

HAFF. She certainly doesn't tell me everything. Well, not immediately. She probably wouldn't have even told me she was pregnant if she hadn't had such a bad day.

ROSE-MARIE. How'd she get pregnant, if you don't mind?...

HAFF. God knows. It's not as if we weren't using every form of birth control ever invented.

ROSE-MARIE. So what are you gonna?...

HAFF. *(crushing a mothball in his fist)* I don't bring it up. It'll just set her off.

(HAFF opens his hand to reveal the crushed mothball.)

HAFF. That's something we could definitely use.

ROSE-MARIE. What's that, Haff?

HAFF. A better mothball.

(LIGHTS DOWN. LIGHTS UP on HAFF, DUNCAN and CRESCENT. DUNCAN looks forlorn.)

HAFF. What's with Duncan?

CRESCENT. He's a little tired. It's a long trip to Attica.

HAFF. He visited his dad.

CRESCENT. You had encouraged them to have some sort of contact.

HAFF. I don't remember doing that.

CRESCENT. He really thinks very highly of you. I think it's a little sad.

HAFF. What?

CRESCENT. That his primary male role model should be the exterminator. I hope you don't take that the wrong way. I didn't mean to say sad, I meant to say... unusual.

HAFF. Well, it is sad.

CRESCENT. *(with a pat on his shoulder before exiting into closet)* He needs a man to man and you're the man.

HAFF. *(approaching DUNCAN)* How are you, Duncan?

DUNCAN. *(downbeat)* O.K.

HAFF. So what's up?

DUNCAN. Nothing.

HAFF. O.K.

DUNCAN. A senior tried to make me eat his infested varsity sweater.

HAFF. We're all working on the problem.

DUNCAN. Don't you get it? It is out of control!

HAFF. No, it isn't.

DUNCAN. You're in denial.

HAFF. So how did it go?

(Pause.)

HAFF. O.K. I'm out of here. I don't have time to pull teeth.

DUNCAN. We had nothing to say.

HAFF. You and your dad?

DUNCAN. He's not my dad. A dad is someone you know. This is a strange man behind glass.

HAFF. They have partitions?

DUNCAN. I didn't mind that part at all. Is the reason they do that so that you can't touch each other?

HAFF. I guess.

DUNCAN. That is a really good idea. I wouldn't want him trying to kiss me or hug me. He wanted to know how I was doing in school.

HAFF. Seems like a fair question. How are you doing?

DUNCAN. I told him about the senior trying to stuff his sweater down my throat. He didn't understand.

HAFF. It's not an easy thing to explain.

DUNCAN. Violence, he gets. He's doing twenty five to life at a maximum security prison for offing mom. I meant my mother. I didn't know her either.

HAFF. What did you ask him?

DUNCAN. If he had a boyfriend.

HAFF. Why would you ask him that?

DUNCAN. I didn't really. It was on a whole list of things I wanted to know but was afraid to ask, topped by why did you shoot her?

HAFF. You know the circumstances.

DUNCAN. Why didn't he shoot the man instead of her?

HAFF. You ask him that?

(DUNCAN shakes his head.)

HAFF. It's probably just as well.

DUNCAN. He's just a stranger. I know you better than I know him and you're my exterminator.

(Impulsively, DUNCAN hugs HAFF, who breaks away.)

HAFF. Hey...

DUNCAN. Sorry. What a crazy thing to do... hug the bug man.

HAFF. Look, you're kind of stressed and depressed and all that.

DUNCAN. Will you still come back?

HAFF. Exterminators always come back, kid.

DUNCAN. *(mostly to himself)* I guess they do, but when the moths are gone, it won't be the same. It'll just be a little spritz once a month and that's it.

(Pause.)

HAFF. Hey, you want to rent *Mothra* sometime?

DUNCAN. What is it?

HAFF. Are you shitting me, Duncan?

DUNCAN. No.

HAFF. You've never seen *Mothra* or *Mosura* (that's the original Japanese title)?

DUNCAN. What is it? One of those old movies where an evil monster destroys Tokyo?

HAFF. Of course she destroys Tokyo. They all do, but there's a reason for it. Mothra is good and she's pretty and she is a goddess.

DUNCAN. Tell me the story.

HAFF. Wouldn't you rather see it?

DUNCAN. Tell me the story and I'll decide if I want to see it.

(The lights go down, except for a spot on DUNCAN and HAFF. Appropriate soundtrack music accompanies HAFF as he narrates the story to a rapt DUNCAN.)

HAFF. Shipwreck survivors are found on Beiru, an island previously used for atomic tests.

DUNCAN. Where's the island?

HAFF. In a mythical place off the coast of Japan. The survivors were protected from radiation by a special juice given to them by the natives. A joint expedition of Japanese and Rolithican scientists arrives on Beiru.

DUNCAN. Is Rolithican mythical too?

HAFF. Probably. The scientists find a pair of fairies.

DUNCAN. Homos?

HAFF. No. Women, little women, very little women, about a foot high. Clark Nelson, he's the leader of the expedition, abducts the little women and puts them in vaudeville...

DUNCAN. Where's vaudeville?

HAFF. You don't need to know. Do you want to hear the story or not?

DUNCAN. Want to.

HAFF. The women sing a song, a sweet song. It sounds almost like a lullaby, which is really a secret distress call to Mothra, a giant caterpillar, regarded as a goddess: O Mothra, hear our plea for you to save us! Over land! Over sea! Like a wave you come. Our guardian angel. Mothra does hear their song. She turns into a moth and flies to rescue the fairies and despite her destruction of the Japanese countryside and a great deal of Tokyo, it is clear that she is fundamentally a well-meaning moth.

DUNCAN. How does she destroy everything?

HAFF. *(demonstrating)* She flaps her wings.

DUNCAN. Cool! Do they shoot her down at the end?

HAFF. I don't want to give everything away.

DUNCAN. *(flapping his "wings")* Moths are so... misunderstood, especially when they're goddesses.

(LIGHTS DOWN. HAFF *comes through closet door, joining* LENAH.)

(LENAH *hugs* HAFF, *backs away from him.*)

HAFF. Do I smell bad or something?

LENAH. You're an exterminator. You always smell bad.

HAFF. Rose-Marie always wears lots of perfume or something. She always smells good.

LENAH. Too much perfume makes me want to vomit. I'd like to meet her sometime.

HAFF. I keep meaning to have her over. You might even like each other.

LENAH. I would like to have more friends, women friends. You're the only one I can talk to.

HAFF. How come you don't have friends at work?

LENAH. It's very tense... intense.

HAFF. Could I just ask you something?

LENAH. Yes.

(Pause.)

HAFF. I just... I just want to know. Have... have you done it yet? *(Pause.)* Do you know what I'm referring to?

LENAH. Can't you tell?

HAFF. Am I supposed to be able to?

LENAH. I don't know.

HAFF. If I could tell, I wouldn't have to ask.

(HAFF goes to LENAH, presses his ear against her stomach.)

LENAH. Haff...

HAFF. I don't hear anything, but I don't know if I'm supposed to hear anything. Probably too early or if it isn't there anymore, too late.

LENAH. There's nothing inside me now.

HAFF. I think I do hear something.

LENAH. I'm hungry. That was just a pang. That's all.

(Lights starts to fade. Stage moth flutters near LENAH's mouth. She tries to push it away but it lingers. LIGHTS UP on HAFF and ROSE-MARIE. ROSE-MARIE is nervously reviewing notes on index cards.)

ROSE-MARIE. I've never spoken publicly before.

HAFF. You'll be swell. The guys are very interested in you.

ROSE-MARIE. That's because I'm the only one who isn't... a guy. I really thought there'd be some other women exterminators at this convention but all the women that I think are exterminators are only exterminators' wives or girlfriends.

HAFF. A lot of exterminators are divorced.

ROSE-MARIE. I wonder why.

HAFF. A lot of everybody is divorced. Maybe you'll meet somebody.

ROSE-MARIE. I have no interest in meeting anybody. This dude tried to tell me he'd exterminated tarantulas in an orchard. I think he was just

Act Two 53

trying to seduce me. I just want to tell them about "The Reemergence of the Clothes Moth in the Twenty First Century" and what to do about it. Do you think they'll care?

HAFF. Every place has the potential for infestation.

ROSE-MARIE. Just because there are no clothes moths in the closets of New Orleans today, doesn't mean there won't be holes in their cardigans come next spring.

HAFF. I've come to a very important decision, Rose-Marie.

ROSE-MARIE. What's that?

HAFF. I want to contribute. I mean it's not going to happen with Lenah. We're not going to have…

ROSE-MARIE. I understand.

HAFF. But I want it to be totally…

(Pause.)

HAFF. Anonymously. Totally anonymously.

ROSE-MARIE. I absolutely agree with you.

HAFF. Nobody must know.

ROSE-MARIE. That's what totally anonymously means.

HAFF. Not even the child.

ROSE-MARIE. That'll be fine.

HAFF. I don't even want to babysit or anything like that. Ever.

ROSE-MARIE. No problem.

HAFF. But you can show me things, if you want or if we're not together, not working together, send me things.

ROSE-MARIE. Why wouldn't we be…

HAFF. You may want to go out on your own or go to college like you said to become a chemist.

ROSE-MARIE. Yes. I see no problem with an arrangement like that.

HAFF. We could even draw something up.

ROSE-MARIE. We seem to be in complete agreement about what we want.

HAFF. I want to leave a part of me behind.

ROSE-MARIE. But you don't want to have any part of it.

HAFF. I guess that's one way of looking at it.

ROSE-MARIE. It's O.K., Haff. We don't want the same things at all, but what you want fits perfectly together with what I want.

HAFF. So when would we want to do it?

ROSE-MARIE. Excuse me?

(At a loss for words, HAFF gestures unintelligibly.)

ROSE-MARIE. Haff, you do understand that this is going to be performed in vitro.

HAFF. Oh sure. I just forgot the word for it. In vitro. What happens? Do I just put my donation in a paper cup or something?

ROSE-MARIE. I'm not actually sure where you put it, Haff. Somebody will show you where to put it.

HAFF. There's absolutely nothing wrong with what we're doing.

ROSE-MARIE. Not from my point of view.

HAFF. It's not like we were having...

ROSE-MARIE. We just went over that.

HAFF. So you want to shake on it?

ROSE-MARIE. Sure. We can shake.

HAFF. Nothing ever wrong with a shake.

(HAFF and ROSE-MARIE join in an extremely warm handshake, which is still in progress as the lights go down. LIGHTS UP on HAFF, DUNCAN and CRESCENT. HAFF takes Mothra tape out of VCR and places it in its cover.)

DUNCAN. Wow.

HAFF. Like it?

Act Two

DUNCAN. I'll say! So they don't kill Mothra at the end.

CRESCENT. What an attractive monster she is. Not exactly sweet or gentle but no Godzilla except I guess they're both Japanese.

DUNCAN. Monsters don't have nationalities.

HAFF. There's a bunch of sequels.

CRESCENT. We'll have many more nights of horror to look forward to.

HAFF. You put the cage outside. I'll be back in the morning to see what happened.

(LIGHTS DOWN.)

NEWSCASTER'S VOICE. And now the latest in what pest professionals are calling the Great Moth Infestation of 2003. Rumors that geckos and ferrets are useful exterminators are not reliable. The Pest Control Board warns against unleashing these creatures in your closets. They will only add to the havoc. Residents should also keep yarn balls away from cats and kittens for the foreseeable future. "There's no sense in having any unnecessary wool," said one reliable source. Let your pets play with plastic.

(LIGHTS UP on HAFF, DUNCAN and CRESCENT around a cage. CRESCENT wears red pajamas.)

HAFF. So what happened? Anything?

DUNCAN. Nothing.

HAFF. She didn't attract any male moths during the night?

CRESCENT. That can happen. Can't it?

DUNCAN. I knew nothing would happen.

HAFF. It worked when I was a kid.

DUNCAN. That was ages ago, Haff, and the city is different.

HAFF. It's got nothing to do with the city. Don't blame it on the city.

DUNCAN. I can order a male on-line or just forget about it.

HAFF. You give up so easily. What if I gave up just because I couldn't make a place rat free the first time around? The only way you fail is to give up.

CRESCENT. Poor Little Miss Mosura. Even if you're descended from a goddess, nobody wants to make love to you.

DUNCAN. She's not descended from anybody. She's just a stupid online ordered moth. Why am I doing this anyhow?

HAFF. Don't you know?

DUNCAN. It's the whole life cycle and you can watch it. And it all happens so fast. You hatch and you immediately prepare to mate because whether you know it or not, life is short.

CRESCENT. It is. Terribly terribly...

DUNCAN. After the male has mated, his purpose in life is done.

CRESCENT. It is.

HAFF. From each egg comes a tiny caterpillar. The baby caterpillars do nothing but eat and eat and eat.

CRESCENT. I'd be pleased to fix you a nice breakfast, Haff.

HAFF. During this time, it will shed its skin four times.

DUNCAN. It gets fat.

HAFF. And when fat, it stops eating and starts spinning.

DUNCAN. The amazing and beautiful metamorphosis often begins with diarrhea.

CRESCENT. That's... fascinating but more information than we really need to know.

HAFF. Now they begin to build their cocoons. In time, the cocoon will hatch an adult moth.

CRESCENT. *(peering into cage)* How's he supposed to get to her?

HAFF. The cage holes are large enough for the tips of the male's abdomen to poke through.

CRESCENT. Maybe she attracted a male with a large... tip.

DUNCAN. Is that possible, Haff?

HAFF. I wouldn't know.

CRESCENT. Maybe they tried, poor things, but were just defeated by the barriers, so he flew away leaving her... frustrated.

DUNCAN. Can't we just put her out again tomorrow night?

HAFF. Sure.

DUNCAN. Will you come back?

HAFF. You know how to do it, Duncan. You don't need me.

CRESCENT. Haff was kind enough to spend last night with us. He shared this beautiful horror movie. We can't expect much more than that.

DUNCAN. Why can't we?

CRESCENT. Duncan, he's the exterminator.

DUNCAN. He's more than that. Aren't you, Haff?

HAFF. I got to go.

CRESCENT. How about that big breakfast I promised you?

DUNCAN. She makes croissants. It's one of the best things Auntie Crescent does. Croissants.

HAFF. I really don't have time for croissants.

CRESCENT. What about eggs?

(They look to the cage.)

HAFF. We still have a situation here with clothes moths.

CRESCENT. We are free of them.

HAFF. Others are not so fortunate.

CRESCENT. French toast really doesn't take very long and everybody likes it.

DUNCAN. I love it! I keep asking for it and never get it, but you CAN GET IT.

HAFF. My fiancée and I have Total and strawberries every morning.

DUNCAN. Boring.

CRESCENT. Bland. Well, thank you for showing us your monster.

DUNCAN. Yeah, thanks. And the movie was so good. I want to see all the sequels in order.

HAFF. Put her cage out again tonight. Maybe something will happen.

(HAFF exits.)

DUNCAN. Nothing is going to happen.

CRESCENT. You expect too much, Duncan.

DUNCAN. I want too much. I don't expect anything.

CRESCENT. He's engaged.

DUNCAN. He never talks about her.

CRESCENT. He just did.

DUNCAN. He talked about their cereal.

CRESCENT. Duncan, the man is not interested in me.

DUNCAN. How do you know?

CRESCENT. I just do. A woman knows. We spent the night… the evening together.

DUNCAN. But you're interested in him.

CRESCENT. He's a nice guy. I don't know much about him other than his interest in bugs. He didn't even say anything about my new red pajamas.

DUNCAN. What did you expect him to say?

CRESCENT. I was going to show him how they were wool, how I bought wool pajamas because I had faith in his ability. Men like to hear how good they are. You're the one who's really interested in him.

DUNCAN. What's that supposed to mean?

CRESCENT. You want him to be your father. That's obvious.

DUNCAN. You only get one father. Mine's in the Big House.

CRESCENT. Someday…

DUNCAN. Don't tell me someday I'll grow up and meet somebody and fall in love and get married and have children. It is not going to happen to me.

CRESCENT. Why couldn't it?

DUNCAN. Because I'm like you. *(indicating cage)* Like her. Not everybody mates. That's a fact of life, auntie.

(LIGHTS DOWN. LIGHTS UP on LENAH, ROSE-MARIE and HAFF. ROSE-MARIE does not appear pregnant in this scene. LENAH is bordering on out of control.)

LENAH. I'm so pleased to finally meet you, Rosemary.

ROSE-MARIE. It's Rose-Marie.

LENAH. I'm sorry. Isn't that what I said?

ROSE-MARIE. I thought you said Rosemary.

LENAH. I completely understand. Most people get my name wrong.

ROSE-MARIE. Lena?

LENAH. There's an "H" at the end of it.

ROSE-MARIE. Oh.

HAFF. Which doesn't really change how you say it, only how you spell it.

LENAH. Oh but it does change it. With an "H" at the end, you need to draw it out a little more. Lenaaah. Lenaah.

HAFF. Do I draw it out?

LENAH. Not as much as you used to. Haff, why don't you fix Rose-Marie a drink.

ROSE-MARIE. Oh, no thanks.

LENAH. Haff, didn't you invite your associate for drinks?

HAFF. You said you wanted to meet Rose-Marie.

LENAH. I said, invite her over for drinks. You weren't expecting dinner were you? Because there is none. Not even Triscuits and cheese. No food.

ROSE-MARIE. Oh no. I wasn't expecting...

LENAH. Something soft.

ROSE-MARIE. What?

LENAH. To drink.

ROSE-MARIE. Sure. That'll be fine.

LENAH. Haff, would you mind preparing the Dr. Ps, sweet thing?

(LENAH *opens a closet door.* HAFF *enters.* LENAH *slams the closet behind him. A few seconds of uncomfortable silence.*)

LENAH. You are so brave.

ROSE-MARIE. Me?

LENAH. Such courage! Most women are nervous and girly about rodents and other vermin. I know I personally am. Do you ever become squeamish? You can tell me. I admire you.

ROSE-MARIE. Haff and I have fewer encounters with actual living rats than you might imagine.

LENAH. I don't imagine anything.

ROSE-MARIE. What is it you do?

LENAH. You don't know what I do? You spend all day spraying poison with my fiancé. Doesn't he ever mention me?

ROSE-MARIE. On occasion you do come up.

LENAH. I'm a 911 dispatcher.

ROSE-MARIE. That's right. I did know that. That must be terribly stressful.

LENAH. It is! I spend all day and sometimes all night needing to know what's really going on in a hurry. Sometimes, it spills over and I end up talking to real people like that, people I know. Of course I don't really know you. This is not an EMERGENCY. This is just Haff's colleague and Diet Dr. Pepper. This is a normal conversation. Are you pregnant?

ROSE-MARIE. Excuse me, Lenaaah.

(*Uncomfortable pause.*)

LENAH. I didn't say that. Could we start over? Talk about the weather? This fog! It seems to last till noon. What's that about? Haff and I love Diet Dr. Pepper with sweet corn on the cob… or anything. It's just amazing we share all of the same favorite things. Like jazz and apricots. What are some of your favorite things, Rosemary... Marie!

ROSE-MARIE. I love my job.

LENAH. And what else? There has got to be something in your life besides extermination.

ROSE-MARIE. Chocolate.

LENAH. I don't ski. Neither does Haff.

ROSE-MARIE. I don't ski either.

LENAH. We all share that, even if it's a common lack of interest.

(HAFF emerges from the closet with the Dr. Peppers.)

LENAH. So if you don't mind my asking. When are you due?

(HAFF nearly drops the Dr. Peppers.)

HAFF. Lenaah!

LENAH. You took so long with those Peppers! Rose-Marie and I are practically girlfriends. Chattering away like baby magpies!

ROSE-MARIE. You told her. I can't believe that you told her.

HAFF. I didn't tell her anything.

LENAH. Haff and I tell each other everything. That's what really close couples do.

ROSE-MARIE. I thought we were in agreement on this.

LENAH. Agreement on what?

ROSE-MARIE. April. That's when I am due.

(ROSE-MARIE takes her Dr. Pepper from HAFF, quaffs it quickly as HAFF and LENAH look on.)

ROSE-MARIE. That's surprisingly... brisk.

LENAH. That's the lemon in the pepper.

HAFF. *(offering seconds)* Another?

ROSE-MARIE. That's Lenah's.

HAFF. Actually, that's mine. Lenah's has extra ice.

LENAH. I've changed my mind. I need something stronger.

(LENAH disappears behind one of the doors.)

HAFF. I really didn't say anything.

ROSE-MARIE. Do you think I'm showing? It's way too early for that.

HAFF. I don't see showing unless it's really obvious. Lenah is pretty observant. What do you think of her?

ROSE-MARIE. I think she makes me nervous. I think I better be going.

HAFF. You just got here. You don't like Lenah? That was fast.

ROSE-MARIE. I didn't say I didn't like her. I said she makes me...

HAFF. She's just like that. You need to get used to her. I'm extremely comfortable with her.

ROSE-MARIE. It would be bad news if you were uncomfortable with someone you were engaged to.

HAFF. She's not like us. She's... complicated.

ROSE-MARIE. We are also complicated.

LENAH. *(reemerging with drink)* Haff and I were also April babies. Not on the same day. We should have been. He was a little early and I was late. Maybe that's why we share so much in common. We're not having any children.

ROSE-MARIE. Yes, that's common knowledge.

LENAH. It's nobody's business really. If we choose to get married and not have children. Just like it's nobody's business if you choose to have children and not get married.

HAFF. Rose-Marie has to go.

LENAH. The restroom is to your left. I cleaned it just for you.

HAFF. I mean she has to leave.

LENAH. I should never have asked when you were due. It was too soon.

ROSE-MARIE. I have class.

LENAH. Oh, do you?

ROSE-MARIE. Chemistry.

LENAH. Oh... school.

ROSE-MARIE. It's very difficult. I thought I'd be good at it, but it's a struggle.

LENAH. Are you thinking of dropping out?

ROSE-MARIE. Sometimes.

LENAH. You'll soon have another mouth to feed.

ROSE-MARIE. I'm not thinking of leaving my job. I love exterminating.

HAFF. Rose-Marie wants to invent a better mothball.

LENAH. Don't you mean a better mousetrap?

ROSE-MARIE. I wouldn't mind doing that either, anything to help humanely rid us of our pests.

LENAH. I don't understand. How is extermination humane?

HAFF. I'm sure when Rose-Marie said humanely...

LENAH. When you kill some vermin, it's perfectly acceptable. It doesn't need to be humane. It's not like they're dogs or people.

ROSE-MARIE. I don't know why I said humanely.

LENAH. It probably made you feel better. Everybody needs to feel good about themselves. Sometimes, you spend all day trying to help others and you come home and you still feel lousy.

ROSE-MARIE. It was nice meeting you... at last.

LENAH. We're getting married on February 29th.

ROSE-MARIE. Oh that's unusual. Well, see you at work tomorrow, Haff.

HAFF. Take care, Rose-Marie.

LENAH. Yes, do. You can never be too careful with children. Even before they're born, whatever you do, affects them.

(ROSE-MARIE *exits through one of the closet doors.*)

LENAH. So who's the father?

HAFF. He's actually... anonymous.

LENAH. She doesn't know.

HAFF. Nobody knows. That's what anonymous means. It's in vitro. You know what that means?

LENAH. Vaguely.

HAFF. You want me to tell you about it.

LENAH. Not particularly.

HAFF. Why are you so interested?...

LENAH. It's hard to know what to talk about with new people.

HAFF. Shouldn't be. You talk to strangers all day.

LENAH. We never have to search for a conversation. We talk about what they want to talk about, what they need to talk about. They are having a heart attack. They have been beaten up. Their daddy isn't moving. Their house is on fire. They are experiencing certain symptoms. They have been or are in the process of being sexually violated. Their dog ate poison. There is a terrorist in their closet. There is blood on their stairwell. They are barely breathing. There's a strange man on their roof. Whatever. It's all about them. Sometimes, it's easier to talk to strangers.

HAFF. She's only been pregnant for like seven weeks or something.

LENAH. Are you sure? She was so obviously showing. That's why I brought it up. Should I apologize?

HAFF. Why should you apologize?

LENAH. I will if you want me to. She's your friend.

HAFF. She's my partner.

LENAH. Partner. I thought she was under you.

HAFF. She got promoted.

LENAH. When did this happen?

HAFF. She's not exactly my partner.

LENAH. She's just no longer exactly under you.

HAFF. Well...

LENAH. And now, if you don't mind, I would like for you to tell me what happened in Cincinnati.

HAFF. Cincinnati.

LENAH. Yes. Cincinnati. The national exterminating convention.

HAFF. I didn't think you were interested in new ways to discourage termites.

LENAH. I'm not.

HAFF. Or how scorpions have suddenly returned to South Carolina in unprecedented numbers.

LENAH. I'm not.

HAFF. Or guaranteed ways to kill gophers.

LENAH. I'm not.

HAFF. Of course, Rose-Marie delivered her speech about moths returning to our nation's closets.

LENAH. Now I'm interested.

HAFF. Well, why didn't you ask her about her speech? It was very well received. She got the biggest hand.

LENAH. Didn't you say she was the only woman?

HAFF. Yes.

LENAH. Do you think that might have had something to do with the size of her hand?

HAFF. I think that she gave exterminators from coast to coast some vital information on the reemergence of the clothes moth after nearly half a century of dormancy.

LENAH. Dormancy, huh?

HAFF. Dormant is inactive, sleeping.

LENAH. Were you dormant with Rose-Marie in Cincinnati?

HAFF. Oh, come on, Lenah, you know me better...

LENAH. Did she sleep with anyone in Cincinnati?

HAFF. Rose-Marie isn't like that.

LENAH. Like what?

HAFF. Somebody who has casual sex at conventions.

LENAH. Well, I know you're not like that.

HAFF. Then why did you ask me if I dormezed with her.

LENAH. Because you're hiding something.

HAFF. You're really good.

LENAH. So, are you going to tell me?

HAFF. It's not what you think.

LENAH. I don't like pulling teeth, Haff. I'm used to extracting information very quickly, though not necessarily painlessly from people I don't know and don't care about.

HAFF. It's just that... well... I'm anonymous.

LENAH. You're anonymous.

HAFF. I was just helping Rose-Marie out. She was looking for an anonymous donor.

LENAH. But you're not anonymous.

HAFF. Not any more. Now that you know.

LENAH. You were never anonymous. She always knew who the father of her child was.

HAFF. I'm not the father.

LENAH. Oh, yes you are.

HAFF. Oh, no I'm not.

LENAH. Then who is?

HAFF. Nobody. Anonymous.

LENAH. And when your son asks…

HAFF. Not my son!

LENAH. Or your daughter asks…

HAFF. He or she is not going to ask me because I am not going to have any contact whatsoever with him or her.

LENAH. Then you can't have any contact with Rose-Marie.

HAFF. Why not?

LENAH. Because it will be too irresistible for you, Haff. I know you. Better than you know yourself.

HAFF. What an arrogant thing to say!

LENAH. And of course you've broken our agreement.

HAFF. I don't see it that way.

LENAH. We agreed not to have any children.

HAFF. Yes.

LENAH. That doesn't mean that we can have them with other people.

HAFF. Like I said, I'm just helping a friend out.

LENAH. Now she's a friend.

HAFF. Yes. A business associate and also a friend.

LENAH. It is a violation.

HAFF. A violation?

LENAH. Of our agreement.

HAFF. I don't think so.

LENAH. Certainly of the spirit of our agreement. You promised me you didn't want any children.

HAFF. I don't!

LENAH. You have a funny way of showing it, by getting somebody pregnant.

HAFF. The only person I got pregnant was you. And that was a miracle... an accidental miracle.

LENAH. Look what he calls it. A miracle! As if it were a blessing.

HAFF. It was a miracle. And you didn't bother telling me when you got rid of it.

LENAH. Well, I did.

HAFF. Obviously.

LENAH. Did you think that I wouldn't?

HAFF. No!

LENAH. Why did you do this?

HAFF. I just wanted to leave something behind.

LENAH. Someone, Haff, some breathing, growing, walking, pissing thing.

HAFF. Someone that I have no responsibility for.

LENAH. You think you have no responsibility for someone you create.

HAFF. About as much as God has.

LENAH. God! God!

HAFF. Rose-Marie and I have an agreement.

LENAH. We had an agreement.

HAFF. We're clear.

LENAH. NO CHILDREN! NO CHILDREN! NO CHILDREN!

HAFF. Well, it's done.

LENAH. So are we.

HAFF. Why?

LENAH. Because I will not be a mother and I will not marry a man who is a father of any kind.

HAFF. I could talk to Rose-Marie.

LENAH. I wish you had talked to me.

HAFF. It's not too late for her to start over.

LENAH. She's not going to have an abortion.

HAFF. Why wouldn't she?

LENAH. For starters, she's Catholic.

HAFF. How do you know that?

LENAH. It's obvious. And she has a thing for you.

HAFF. Rose-Marie does not have a thing!

LENAH. I'm not saying for sure but there's a very good chance that she's in love with you.

HAFF. I love you, just you. Lenaah!

LENAH. I didn't say you're in love with her. But somehow she's got it in the back of her head that it could all work out. You and Rose-Marie and baby makes three.

HAFF. She knows I'm engaged.

LENAH. I couldn't possibly marry you. All we'd wind up doing is getting a divorce.

HAFF. Why?

LENAH. Because deep in our hearts, we want different things.

HAFF. Shit! I should never have agreed to this.

LENAH. You want to be a daddy.

HAFF. Agreeing to be her anonymous. It was wrong. I am completely and totally wrong.

LENAH. It's good this betrayal came out now.

HAFF. It's not good! It's terrible! It's not betrayal! It's misunderstanding! We've got to talk this over.

LENAH. I'll talk to you, Haff, for a while, until I get tired of it, but it's not going to change anything, so really what's the use of a lot of talk.

HAFF. Talking does change things.

LENAH. Not something like this. You either want to be a parent or you don't and I don't.

HAFF. And I don't.

LENAH. And I don't believe you.

HAFF. I swear it! I swear it!

LENAH. I don't want to have one growing inside me, adopt one, be responsible for one. I think a family can be just one man and one woman and no pabulum and a lot less pain and disillusionment. You know where I've been and how I feel.

LENAH. Please don't kiss me now.

HAFF. I wasn't going to.

LENAH. Oh, yes you were. I know that look, that kiss look.

HAFF. I was just thinking. Should I? Would that help?

LENAH. No.

HAFF. That's what I thought. So I didn't. I'm sensitive. You have to agree, as men go.

LENAH. Like I said, before you, I mostly went with cops.

HAFF. I don't ever want to be totally responsible for another person. And you have to be with children. It's pretty risky and I don't want to take that risk. Most people think it's worth it. I don't.

LENAH. But you do, Haff, and if I deprive you of it, you will resent me, and I couldn't bear that, not from you, not from such a good man.

HAFF. It's not that you don't want to have children, you don't want to have anyone, Lenah. Is that how you feel?

LENAH. At the moment.

HAFF. So you'd like me to leave.

LENAH. Please. Yes.

HAFF. You would really like me to leave?

(LENAH snaps her fingers.)

HAFF. I guess we no longer agree about everything.

LENAH. We never really did. That was silly, Haff. You really should be a father, a man like you.

HAFF. I don't want to be.

LENAH. You think about it. Think hard.

HAFF. I have. I haven't changed my mind. We still feel the same way about that.

LENAH. Then I don't trust the way you feel.

HAFF. You don't trust anybody.

LENAH. I don't even trust myself.

(LENAH *touches* HAFF's *cheek very lightly. The lights, except for an intensely bright spot on them, go down. A stage moth flies between them.*)

LENAH. Aren't you going to kill it?

HAFF. No.

LENAH. Isn't that what you do?

HAFF. This kind of moth, the kind that is attracted to light, is harmless.

LENAH. Aren't you going to kill it anyway?

HAFF. I've been killing all day. If it's bothering you, you kill it. You don't need a professional.

LENAH. I don't want to kill anything else.

(HAFF *hugs her.* LENAH *kisses* HAFF. *LIGHTS DOWN. LIGHTS UP on* HAFF *and* ROSE-MARIE *going in and out of closet doors with flashlights, always missing each other. When he is in one closet, she emerges from another one. LIGHTS DOWN. LIGHTS UP on* LENAH.)

LENAH. 911. What's your emergency?

(*LIGHTS UP on* CRESCENT *in her red pajamas.*)

CRESCENT. A missing child.

LENAH. Your child?

CRESCENT. I am his guardian.

LENAH. How old is the child?

CRESCENT. Duncan is sixteen.

LENAH. How long has he been missing?

CRESCENT. He never came home from school.

LENAH. When?

CRESCENT. Today.

LENAH. That's seven hours. A sixteen year old boy cannot be missing after seven hours. He's probably with a friend.

CRESCENT. He doesn't have any friends.

LENAH. Call your local precinct if he's still missing after twenty four hours. Yours is not an official emergency, ma'am.

CRESCENT. He is often bullied. What if his tormenters have gone too far? What if they've killed him?

LENAH. In that circumstance, you may call 911. You would then have an official emergency.

CRESCENT. Thank you. I'll call back if my nephew has been murdered. His mother was. Well, you don't care, you cold-hearted person. What if your kid didn't come home?

(LIGHTS go quickly DOWN on CRESCENT, as she turns revealing holes in her pajama bottoms.)

(LIGHTS UP on HAFF. He opens a closet door to reveal DUNCAN.)

HAFF. Duncan.

DUNCAN. Hi, Haff.

HAFF. Have they come back?

DUNCAN. Who?

HAFF. The clothes moths.

DUNCAN. No. Well, there's nothing woolen left except my aunt's pajamas. We even got rid of our blankets. All we have are comforters.

HAFF. Is this about the other moths, the ones you were trying to mate?

DUNCAN. No. I decided I wasn't interested in mating.

HAFF. Oh.

DUNCAN. Not everything is about moths. Could I maybe stay with you?

HAFF. What?

DUNCAN. Dumb idea, huh?

HAFF. Duncan, I am your exterminator.

DUNCAN. Yeah.

HAFF. People do not stay with their exterminators.

DUNCAN. I thought we were friends.

HAFF. Duncan, men and boys cannot be friends.

DUNCAN. What do you mean?

HAFF. It looks suspicious.

DUNCAN. What? Like you're a perv or something?

HAFF. I am not...

DUNCAN. I know. I wouldn't go somewhere where I'd be... perved.

HAFF. Your aunt...

DUNCAN. Don't say she loves me.

HAFF. She cares about you.

DUNCAN. She's trying to get me a scholarship to military school.

HAFF. Military school?

DUNCAN. In Pennsylvania.

HAFF. What's the point of sending a boy like you to military school?

DUNCAN. She says she's at wit's end. Where's that? Wit's end? Pennsylvania?

HAFF. Don't you have any other relatives?

DUNCAN. Only my father and he can't exactly take me in and when he gets out, I'll be too old to be taken in, not that I'd want to stay with him, even if he wasn't in maximum security.

HAFF. I'm really touched, you know, that you should come to me.

DUNCAN. You're the only person I have ever met who gets me.

HAFF. I get some of you.

DUNCAN. The moth part of me.

HAFF. Yeah.

DUNCAN. That's the biggest and the only interesting part of me.

HAFF. It just seems that way. It's because of this situation we're having right now, but it's not going to go on much longer.

DUNCAN. You've killed them all?

HAFF. You can never kill all of any kind of species. If you did, they'd be extinct and you wouldn't want that.

DUNCAN. Most people would want to live in a world devoid of things that eat their clothes and cereal.

HAFF. Where would that leave me?

DUNCAN. Don't worry. It's not going to happen. Exterminators are always going to be necessary. It's not something I'd ever want to do.

HAFF. Most people wouldn't. What would you like to do?

DUNCAN. Something where I wouldn't have to work with people or vermin.

HAFF. Do you want to call your aunt or should I?

(DUNCAN starts to run off. HAFF grabs him.)

DUNCAN. It was nice knowing you.

(DUNCAN offers his hand to HAFF, who takes it. Then hugs him.)

DUNCAN. What's that all about?

HAFF. Just an innocent hug from the bug man.

(DUNCAN *shrugs.*)

HAFF. And thank you.

DUNCAN. For what? What did I do?

HAFF. Nothing bad, kid. Nothing bad.

DUNCAN. You look like you want to hug me again.

HAFF. No. That's enough.

(*They do hug. LIGHTS DOWN. LIGHTS UP on LENAH.*)

LENAH. What's your emergency? ...Your lover is gone? ... When you say gone, do you mean... no, you just mean gone, don't you? I'm so glad you called 911. That was exactly the right thing to do. Tell me all about him, miss. If you cry I can't understand you.... Was he a good man? Was he a caring man? Did he know what he wanted? Did you? ... Don't tell me that, ma'am... I'm afraid I cannot help you if you tell me that. What was she like? This other woman? Is she a warm woman? A giving woman? Are you? ... It should be easy... just to give, but it isn't always, is it? Sometimes, it's such a struggle, just to be kind. Are you still there, ma'am? Where did you go? You and your awful emergency.

(*LIGHTS DOWN. LIGHTS UP on DUNCAN emerging from a closet door. He is hugged by CRESCENT.*)

CRESCENT. You scared the hell out of me, disappearing like that.

DUNCAN. I'm sorry. It was kind of wicked.

CRESCENT. For the first time, I felt like we were flesh and blood, not an aunt's blood, a mother's blood. Don't ever pull a stunt like that again.

DUNCAN. Or it's off to Wit's End, P-A.

CRESCENT. Sit down and eat. What do you want? I know what you want.

DUNCAN. French toast!

CRESCENT. We're out of syrup.

DUNCAN. I'll get some.

CRESCENT. Don't leave. It's so good. It doesn't need any syrup. Syrup just drowns its goodness.

(LIGHTS DOWN. LIGHTS UP on HAFF and ROSE-MARIE, who is extremely pregnant. They emerge from doors.)

ROSE-MARIE. It's amazing.

HAFF. Huh?

ROSE-MARIE. It's been a month since we've had any moth calls.

HAFF. Things have calmed down quite a bit.

ROSE-MARIE. It's funny. Now that the moths have gone, it seems like everything else is back.

HAFF. That's the way cycles are.

ROSE-MARIE. More rats.

HAFF. More mice.

ROSE-MARIE. Even the roaches have returned.

HAFF. They never...

ROSE-MARIE. I know they never really went away, but they've come out of the walls now that the moths have gone wherever it is they go.

HAFF. One thing is certain, people in this city will think twice before they buy wool.

ROSE-MARIE. You think that's a permanent change?

HAFF. I think people are comfortable with their acrylics. Why risk wool?

ROSE-MARIE. Sometimes, risk is good.

HAFF. But is wool really worth it?

ROSE-MARIE. Wool is real. It feels real. That's important to some people.

HAFF. Don't you think it's time you stopped working?

ROSE-MARIE. I'm O.K.

HAFF. You're about to give birth and you're climbing stairs and you're spraying poison all day.

ROSE-MARIE. I'm only eight months...

HAFF. Only! Being risky with fabric is one thing but walk-ups and insecticides. I am ordering you to stop exterminating.

ROSE-MARIE. Are you speaking as my employer?

HAFF. Yes, and as the baby's...

ROSE-MARIE. That would be a violation of our agreement.

HAFF. Agreement doesn't go into effect until the baby is born.

ROSE-MARIE. We need a written contract.

HAFF. No, we don't.

ROSE-MARIE. We seem to be having a disagreement.

HAFF. Fine. So, let's talk about it.

ROSE-MARIE. I don't like the fact that you're using the fact that you're my boss to tell me what to do in my personal life.

HAFF. That's my kid you're carrying!

ROSE-MARIE. No. It isn't. Try to remember: You are anonymous.

HAFF. Let's end the anonymosity.

ROSE-MARIE. What do you want, Haff?

HAFF. I want... I want... *(pacing)* I want to be a father! A real actual unanonymous father.

ROSE-MARIE. You want to break our agreement.

HAFF. I want to exterminate it.

ROSE-MARIE. And what if the baby is born retarded, deaf, blind with a bad heart or Down's Syndrome.

HAFF. Or all of the above. I will love him or her. I will be responsible.

ROSE-MARIE. What if he or she is a hyperactive obsessive compulsive drug addicted underachieving foul-mouthed surly gay juvenile delinquent?

HAFF. Stuff happens. We will deal with it.

ROSE-MARIE. We?

HAFF. That's the other thing I want. I want us to be a family. Man. Woman. Child. Family. Traditional.

ROSE-MARIE. Aren't you assuming a great deal?

HAFF. Like what?

ROSE-MARIE. Like I love you.

HAFF. Don't you?

ROSE-MARIE. Can't say that I do.

HAFF. Then you don't.

ROSE-MARIE. I would never say that I don't.

HAFF. Then what?

ROSE-MARIE. I feel as though I've turned into the Other Woman and we've never even kissed.

HAFF. Lenah and I weren't right for each other. Just because two people agree about everything doesn't make them right. But she did understand one thing about me, the thing that meant we could never be happy. She was right. I want to be a father and I want everything that comes with it, even if it ruins my life, even if it gives me a whole new life, even if it doesn't make as much difference as I think it's going to make. I do want to be a father. That feeling is growing inside of me in some place that I only just reached. Things can grow in men. It's just not so obvious and frequently, it does not emerge.

ROSE-MARIE. I did not intentionally set a trap for you. I've never even been *the* Woman let alone the Other Woman. I know how to catch rats and mice and a variety of vermin but not men. I did not have a plan to capture you. It was a mistake to request your fertilization.

HAFF. No. It was exactly the right thing to do.

(ROSE-MARIE *pulls* HAFF *towards her, so that he can listen to the baby.*)

ROSE-MARIE. Listen harder, Haff. Think harder. You've got to be sure before you make or break this kind of agreement with someone.

(*There is quiet as* HAFF *listens hard to* ROSE-MARIE's *tummy.*)

HAFF. O.K. I know that now. Ooh.

ROSE-MARIE. What?

HAFF. He moved. Forgive me for saying he.

ROSE-MARIE. There is nothing to forgive. I think it's a boy too.

HAFF. The exterminators' son moved... again.

ROSE-MARIE. Next week, I will stop working but when our child is two months old, I will return to pest control on a part-time basis.

HAFF. I would expect that you would. Your life would be unfulfilled without extermination.

(HAFF continues to listen for sounds of his child. Lights fade to a spot on HAFF and ROSE-MARIE. A stage moth flutters into the light. They pay no attention to it.)

HAFF. Know what I was thinking about?

ROSE-MARIE. What?

HAFF. *Mothra.* You know it?

ROSE-MARIE. Of course I do, silly man. Mightiest monster in all creation! Only she wasn't a monster at all.

HAFF. She was a goddess, a misunderstood goddess.

ROSE-MARIE & HAFF. Mothra! Ravishing a universe for love!

(As the lights begin to fade on HAFF and ROSE-MARIE, the stage moth flies away from them, as the light disappears.)

END OF PLAY

Props

"Stage" moths
Woolen clothing
Notebook and pencil
Moth eaten man's blue suit
Trash bags
Cereal boxes (Cocoa Puffs, Kix, Total, Wheaties)
Sweater with holes
Scarf with holes
Woman's black suit
Giant stage moth
Mothballs
Video tape cassette
Small cage
Dr. Pepper in glasses
Flashlights

Tiger in the Tree

a new play by M. Z. Ribalow

Tiger in the Tree was first presented as a staged reading at EST/Southampton Arts. The cast was Patricia Randell and Alfredo Narciso, and the direction was by Giovanna Sardelli. The playwright would like to acknowledge the invaluable help of New River Dramatists in developing this play. The play is dedicated, with unwavering love, to Donna Jo Davis.

Characters

NANCY—An irresistible woman.
JOSE—Latino, literate, educated, driven.

Place: A house near Grassy Creek in rural North Carolina.
Time: Now.

ACT I
Scene One

(A house. Night. Dark, but we can see well enough by the moonlight outside. A woman enters from the outside, closing the door softly behind her. She looks around as if she has at last entered a place of which she has long dreamed. She goes to an easy chair and sits in it. Suddenly a light snaps on, and a man stands by an inside door. He is rumpled, as if he has just awakened. He blinks against the light, and seems tense. He holds a gun in his hand, and makes sure she sees it as he points it at her.)

JOE. Don't move.

NANCY. *(utterly calm)* Why would I want to move?

JOE. This is a gun, you know.

NANCY. A .38 Special.

JOE. It's loaded.

NANCY. It wouldn't be much use if it wasn't.

JOE. I'll shoot if I have to.

NANCY. You don't have to.

JOE. Just stay there.

NANCY. Thank you. I do feel rather at peace here.

JOE. While I call the police.

NANCY. Oh, you won't do that.

JOE. Won't I?

NANCY. No.

JOE. Why not?

NANCY. You don't want the publicity.

JOE. You know who I am.

NANCY. I do, yes.

JOE. The police are friends of mine. They'd keep it quiet.

NANCY. I could ruin your reputation, and your life, by simply going public. I could sell my story to the *New York Post*— they have it in for you anyway, since that premiere where you knocked them for their mindless attacks on Alec Baldwin.

JOE. You could sell *what* story?

NANCY. How you invited me up here and forced yourself on me against my will. That'd do ghastly things to your image, wouldn't it? Think how much that would alienate your female readers.

JOE. You'd have no proof. Since there isn't any.

NANCY. Don't be silly. I know every detail of your body. And of this house. And there are all the incriminating photos I could create through the wonders of modern technology. So I very much doubt your pals on the force could keep this one quiet. No matter how friendly Dave and Randy act with you.

JOE. You know them?

NANCY. I know who they are.

JOE. Then they know who *you* are.

NANCY. *Do* they?

JOE. Look. I don't want any trouble with you.

NANCY. I don't want any trouble with you, either.

JOE. If you leave now, we'll forget the whole thing.

NANCY. But I just arrived.

JOE. Listen, Ms....

NANCY. McGill. Lil McGill.

JOE. Ms. McGill.

NANCY. But you can call me Nancy.

JOE. Very funny. Ms. McGill...

NANCY. Nancy.

JOE. You obviously know who I am. But I don't know who *you* are, or why you're here.

NANCY. I'm an avid student of your *oeuvre*.

JOE. Ah. I see.

NANCY. You don't, yet. But you will.

JOE. I'll be glad to autograph a picture for you.

NANCY. I already know what you look like.

JOE. Or a book.

NANCY. Read them all already.

JOE. I'll even sign my full name. I don't do that for anyone.

NANCY. You did it for your mother, when your first novel was published.

JOE. You *have* done your homework.

NANCY. Better than you know, Jose.

JOE. Joe. Just plain Joe.

NANCY. But you'd sign it "Jose." Your full name, right?

JOE. Right. Just for you, Ms. McGill. Jose Antonio Ramirez Escalante Reyes.

NANCY. Valdez.

JOE. Excuse me?

NANCY. Jose Antonio Ramirez Escalante Valdez Reyes. You left out the Valdez.

JOE. How do you know... *(beat)* No one knows that.

NANCY. *I* do.

JOE. That is no longer part of my name. Not for a very long time.

NANCY. I know. Not since your uncle Ramon did all those terrible things to you.

(Joe stares at her, disoriented.)

NANCY. I told you. I've studied you as thoroughly as one can a subject. You're my specialty.

JOE. You amaze me, Ms. McGill.

NANCY. Nancy.

JOE. I really think...

NANCY. Nancy. Don't fight it, Joe.

JOE. What is it you want, Nancy?

NANCY. You can put the gun down.

JOE. For all I know, *you* might have one.

NANCY. For all you know. But I don't. I don't need a gun.

(He hesitates, then puts it on a table where he can easily reach it if he wants to.)

JOE. What *do* you want?

NANCY. I want only the best for you. Always.

JOE. So?

NANCY. So I'm worried about you.

JOE. Worried?

NANCY. Perhaps concerned is a better word. Yes. I'm concerned about you, Joe.

JOE. Why?

NANCY. You're not taking full advantage of all the opportunities you've been given. You're beginning to settle for satisfaction instead of striving for fulfillment.

JOE. Thanks. I'll watch out for that.

NANCY. Just sleep, relax and focus on the new book. Swim your forty laps at the pool. Why get to thirty-six and *then* quit, the way you did yesterday?

JOE. How do you know how many laps I've been swimming? Are you following me?

NANCY. And just forget Alison. She was a bitch anyway. You can do better than her. Easily.

(Joe looks at her in absolute shock. Beat.)

JOE. Alison was a secret.

NANCY. You have no secrets from me.

JOE. Alison had a sweet nature and a generous spirit.

NANCY. She had the tits of a starlet, the legs of a runway model, and the mind of a child. You're depressed because she's gone, but you'd be just as depressed if she was still here. Remember how edgy you were getting with her before she finally left? She was giving your headaches, headaches.

JOE. You can't possibly know... *(pause)* And I feel perfectly healthy.

NANCY. Then why take all that Vicodin and Excedrin? And how many times did you suddenly feel dizzy last week? Two? Or three?

JOE. *Dios mio...* you got this place bugged or something?

NANCY. Of course not. I'm just explaining why I'm so concerned about you. I'm right, aren't I? I always am. Sometimes it seems more a curse than a blessing.

JOE. I think you should go now. Let me get back to sleep.

NANCY. Aren't you going to offer me a cup of that delicious strawberry tea you import from London?

JOE. Jesus, you know more about me than I do.

NANCY. I do, actually. Oddly exciting, isn't it?

JOE. You think so?

NANCY. Sure. You're intrigued by inexplicable phenomena.

JOE. You seem more like a pathetic nutcase than an inexplicable phenomenon.

NANCY. *(beat)* You don't mean that.

JOE. Don't I?

NANCY. Of course not. If you did, you wouldn't be so attracted to me.

JOE. Fuck you.

NANCY. Exactly.

JOE. You're fantasizing, Nancy.

NANCY. Actually, *you're* fantasizing. About me. You have been since the moment you came in and saw me sitting here so at ease in your favorite chair. Imagining what my body would look like, stretched out naked and waiting for you. What it might feel like under you. Over you.

JOE. Look, Nancy, I don't know how to say this politely...

NANCY. No tea?

JOE. No fucking tea. What are you doing here?

NANCY. I came to save you, Joe.

JO. From what?

NANCY. From yourself. You've been making some misguided choices. I can help you make better ones.

JOE. Like *you*?

NANCY. Well. Yes.

JOE. Why are so many people, with their letters and calls and e-mails, so convinced that they are the perfect woman of my dreams?

NANCY. Because they're delusional obsessive lunatics without a real life of their own. The difference between them and me is, I'm right.

JOE. Sure.

NANCY. Well, I'm aware you don't know me as well as you're going to, but you surely realize by now that I'm not, as you put it, a pathetic nutcase. I'm hardly a sad-sack loony like Roberta Bronker.

JOE. How do you?... Oh, never mind.

NANCY. I know all about you, Joe. Have you thought about what that means?

JOE. That you've got a pretty empty life?

NANCY. That I know what you want. And how you like it.

JOE. What do you mean?

NANCY. Think about it. Tempting, isn't it? Sweet.

JOE. Stay away from me.

NANCY. I haven't moved.

JOE. I don't want anything to do with you.

NANCY. Why not? I may be the woman of your dreams.

JOE. You're the woman of my nightmares.

NANCY. Nightmares are dreams, too.

JOE. Look. I don't know you. I don't care about you. I don't want you.

NANCY. You don't know me. You don't care about me. Which only makes it easier for you to want me.

(Joe picks up the gun and holds it as if using it to fend her off.)

NANCY. Which one of us are you trying to excite with that thing?

(Joe hesitates, then puts the gun down again, but keeps it close.)

JOE. What can I offer you to make you go?

NANCY. Your faith. Your trust. Your complete willingness to share yourself with me. Honestly and fully.

JOE. Then you'll go?

NANCY. Then I'll *offer* to go. But you won't want me to by then. You won't *let* me go. Why *would* you?

JOE. Maybe because I want a quiet, normal life with you totally out of it?

NANCY. But you don't want any such thing, or I wouldn't be here. You want to be different. Special. Understood. Loved.

JOE. There are things you don't know about me.

NANCY. Name one.

(He starts to, then stops, realizing he can't say anything; either she knows it already, or he'll be telling her when he says it.)

JOE. I know *nothing* about you.

NANCY. I could be so many different things. And as long as that's true, there's the chance that I'm any or even all of them. Every dark desperate fantasy. Every filthy unspoken desire that's ever grabbed you by the balls and teased them till they were more than ready to burst into pleasure so intense that you can imagine only its blissful pain. Any image that's ever flashed through the most hidden corners of your mind's most secret closets. I may be any of those movies in your mind's screening room. I may be your fantasy film festival.

JOE. Or not.

NANCY. But, Joe.

JOE. What?

NANCY. You're dying of curiosity. Aren't you?

JOE. I can throw you out, you know.

(He takes a step towards her.)

NANCY. Go on. Make me do what you want.

JOE. You think I can't?

NANCY. Impose your will on me.

(Joe starts towards her as if to approach her, but stops and then backs away, uncertain what to do. She remains still, at ease, aware of his every movement, making no attempt to counter anything he does.)

JOE. You little bitch. I ought to...

NANCY. Oh, yes. Anything at all.

JOE. I know what I want.

NANCY. No, you don't.

JOE. And it isn't you.

NANCY. Yes, it is.

JOE. Nancy. Of course, you want to be wanted. And apparently, you want *me* to be the one who wants you. I understand that.

NANCY. Do you?

JOE. But a man has to make his own decision about these things. A man needs to be the pursuer, not the one being pursued.

NANCY. The hunter, not the prey?

JOE. I didn't mean... but, well, yes. If you put it like that.

NANCY. Why are you fighting it so hard?

JOE. Fighting *what*?

NANCY. Your desire for me.

JOE. And what makes you think *you* are my dream girl?

NANCY. I wouldn't be here if I wasn't.

JOE. Nancy... look, you're an intriguing woman, and I am touched, really I am, by your fascination with me — it's flattering, if a bit creepy — and maybe if we'd met in a bar and I felt like buying you a drink, then maybe we would have ended up back here anyway. But under the circumstances...

NANCY. Joe. Remember your train fantasy?

(He stops in his tracks. During the next lines he stands overcome; she is pushing all sorts of secret buttons to which he is quite vulnerable.)

NANCY. What about the classroom fantasy? You had that one quite a bit when you taught those college girls. And don't think for a minute they didn't know what they were doing with those skirts and those open blouses. If they hadn't wanted to be noticed, they wouldn't have dressed — or undressed — that way. Or how about the police station scenario? Or the one about the hitchhiker?

(He stands still, unable to speak. She rises up and gestures to the easy chair.)

NANCY. Sit down.

JOE. Why?

NANCY. Sit. I'm going to do everything you'd like me to. Exactly when and how you want me to. And you won't have to say a word. You see, your fantasies are mine. The same ones. I want exactly what you want. And isn't that what you've always wanted in a woman?

(As if mesmerized, Joe allows her to lead him into the chair. As he is about to sit, he seems to suddenly change his mind and starts to rise. But she gently, seductively, reassuringly, pushes him back into the chair again.)

NANCY. Don't you want to find out what that's like, Joe? Don't you want to know?

(Joe sits, facing us. She stands a few feet away from him, her back to us. She starts to remove her blouse in a sensual manner, as if there is all the time in the world, and there is nothing more important than this moment. Though we don't see her frontally, as he does, we should feel fully his impression that she is irresistibly alluring.)

NANCY. Whatever you're imagining. That's what's going to happen.

JOE. I don't know if...

NANCY. I'm here for you. You can have anything at all. Everything you want. And all you have to do, is just accept it.

JOE. I don't...

(*He seems to drop his resistance, and surrenders to the spell.*)

NANCY. Say my name, Joe.

JOE. What?

NANCY. Say my name, and it's yours. Anything you ever wanted a woman to do to you, without your having to ask. Everything. Just say my name.

JOE. Your name.

NANCY. Say Nancy.

JOE. Nancy.

NANCY. Nancy.

JOE. Nancy.

NANCY. Yes.

(*She is naked from the waist up, her back to us. She drops to her knees and starts to slowly crawl towards him.*)

JOE. Yes.

NANCY. Oh, yes.

JOE. Nancy?

NANCY. Yes.

JOE. There's something I'm not telling you.

(*She regards him. Beat.*)

NANCY. I know.

(*She crawls towards him. He becomes totally passive, letting her have her way. The lights fade to black as the scene ends.*)

ACT I
Scene Two

(Later that night. NANCY and JOE lie on the floor.)

JOE. I have never, and I do mean never, felt anything like that.

NANCY. That's what happens when I do what you want because it's what *I* want, too, not just because it pleases you. Makes a difference, doesn't it?

JOE. Makes *all* the difference.

NANCY. Glad to hear it. Are you ready for more?

JOE. Actually, no, not yet. Got to catch my breath first.

NANCY. Feel free.

JOE. Don't you ever have to catch your breath?

NANCY. Never.

JOE. Never?

NANCY. Caught it long ago. It's there whenever I need it.

(Nancy lights a cigarette.)

JOE. Those things will kill you.

NANCY. No, they won't.

JOE. Nancy?

NANCY. Yes?

JOE. I don't know how to say this.

NANCY. Yes, you do. Or you would never have started the sentence.

JOE. Okay. Then I don't know *whether* to say it.

NANCY. What you *don't* say can be as damaging as what you do. Use the voice you were given.

JOE. All right. *(beat)* I think I love you.

NANCY. You *think*?

JOE. Well, it does seem so ridiculously... premature. I've known you only a few hours. Although it feels as though I've known you my whole life.

NANCY. I feel the same way.

JOE. But — we just met. You broke into my house. You're a complete mystery to me. We've made love *once*.

NANCY. Have we *stopped* doing that?

JOE. That's the point. It feels like... well, love. And how *can* it be?

NANCY. You mean, on such short notice?

JOE. Well...

NANCY. Is there a minimum residency required for the emotion to be validated?

JOE. No, of course not. I believe in love at first sight. Don't you?

NANCY. I believe in love *before* first sight.

JOE. For all I know, you could be dangerous.

NANCY. I'm the most dangerous woman you will ever meet.

JOE. Should I be worried?

NANCY. No.

JOE. Why not?

NANCY. Because I'm on your side.

JOE. I'm not always sure where that is.

NANCY. It doesn't matter. Wherever it is, I'm on it. Even when *you're* not.

JOE. But am I *truly* in love with you? Or is it just... infatuation?

NANCY. What do *you* think?

JOE. I'm lying here, thinking how perfect you are. I expect I'll be fantasizing about you quite a bit in the future.

NANCY. You've done plenty of fantasizing about me in the *past*. You just didn't know who I was.

JOE. That's sort of true, in a way. I've always been in love with the notion of being in love. Do you know what I mean?

(She raises an eyebrow. He almost laughs out loud.)

JOE. Silly question. Of course you do. I loved this perfect woman, you see. Deeply. Passionately.

NANCY. Completely.

JOE. Yes. Completely. But even though she was my dream girl — my true love, my grand passion, my soul mate, my other half — I somehow never knew who she was. Or even what she looked like.

NANCY. And now you do.

JOE. So it seems. But all that time — the years that drifted past, never to return — all those hot lonely nights, I knew she was out there somewhere. I knew that as surely as I knew that there was a heaven above my head, and an earth beneath my feet. I *believed*. If only I could find her; if we could just find each other. No matter how long it took, I had no doubt — not really — that she was The One. If only we could just, finally, meet. I had conviction. I had faith. So I never stopped looking. Which, of course, cost me every relationship I ever did have.

NANCY. Because you never stopped looking.

JOE. Because none of them was ever quite *it*. Consuela came close...

NANCY. I wondered when you were going to bring her up. It wouldn't have worked, Joe. She dreamed of being conventional. Your fantasies were incompatible.

JOE. And Francesca might have...

NANCY. She didn't love you.

JOE. Susie loved me.

NANCY. Susie *loved* you, but she didn't *want* you.

JOE. They were all wonderful creations.

NANCY. They were.

JOE. But they were all — in totally different ways, of course — they were each of them just a bit too...

NANCY. Real?

JOE. That's not very nice.

NANCY. *I'm* not very nice. If I was, I wouldn't seem so perfect to you.

JOE. I don't know what you've done to me...

NANCY. Why do you have to know? Why can't you just *bask* in Paradise, without having to estimate its property value?

JOE. If I ask you a question, will you give me an honest answer?

NANCY. I will *always* give you an honest answer. I just won't always tell you what you want to hear.

JOE. Why do I feel this way with you, and not with any of the others?

NANCY. Haven't you been listening to yourself, Joe? You've spent your life carrying around a glass slipper. And any woman you've ever loved even a little bit, you've tried to make fit into that slipper. And if it was too tight, or too loose, or the instep was even a fraction snug, you measured that foot, and found it... imperfect. One way or another, you found that woman *wanting*. Oh, you let yourself desire her — you even let yourself *love* her — but not absolutely. Not with the abandonment of complete commitment. Not with bottom-of-the-well, heaven-or-hell love. More with... "Love Lite." Genuine enough, but not nearly as profound as it *could* have been. Was that kind? To either one of you?

JOE. You make it sound like...

NANCY. Yes?

JOE. Like I've done something... wrong.

NANCY. Wrong?

JOE. Inappropriate.

NANCY. What's appropriate in love?

JOE. Unkind, then.

NANCY. Well, as we've noted, Joe, you don't *do* kind. Kind is not your forte.

JOE. What did I do that wasn't... honorable?

NANCY. You let them love you.

JOE. So?

NANCY. You let them go further down the path than you were prepared to go yourself. You let them keep going when you were unwilling to join them.

JOE. That was their choice.

NANCY. And *their* problem, yes. But it was your *doing*. And you are responsible for the consequences of what you *do*, don't you think?

JOE. I was just trying...

NANCY. To see who fit the slipper. Yes, I know. But even when you *knew* it wouldn't fit, you kept making her try to wear it.

JOE. I didn't *make* anyone do anything.

NANCY. I don't judge you. I just hold up the mirror and let you see what you are. And what you are not.

JOE. And what are *you*, Nancy?

NANCY. I am The One, Joe. For you. I fit the glass slipper.

JOE. Better than anyone I've ever known.

NANCY. Better than anyone you will *ever* know. Your slipper fits me perfectly. It will *only* fit me.

JOE. You can't be sure of that.

NANCY. Oh, yes I can.

JOE. How?

NANCY. Because the slipper is *mine*. It belongs to me.

JOE. *(beat)* I don't understand quite how you mean that.

NANCY. You will.

JOE. How can I want you so much, when I have no idea at all who you are? How can I love you, when I don't understand the first thing about you? I'm not denying my passion for you, but it makes no sense. Yet — it's the only thing that does. I don't know who you are, or what you want; but I can't imagine a world without you, even though I lived in one before we met. When I yearn now for a touch that will soothe my spirit, make everything all right — or at least seem so — it's you I'll reach for. You I'll write for, when I forge words on a page. You I'll celebrate, when I admire the stars in the sky and try to conjure a comparison. You I want to live for, and die for — even though I don't want to die, not ever.

NANCY. I'd rather be lived for. I've never been impressed by martyrs.

JOE. Your heart — you have a slight arrhythmia, don't you?

NANCY. Atrial Fibrillation.

JOE. So do I. As I'm sure you know. Somehow, I'm keenly aware that your heart skips the same beats as mine. I can *feel* your heart as though it's mine.

NANCY. In a way, it is. Our hearts are one.

JOE. Why do I feel this way, Nancy? How *can* I feel this way?

NANCY. It's called love, my heart. And there's nothing wrong with it.

JOE. Is this what you want?

NANCY. This is what I am.

(They kiss. Passionately. Eternally. Lights fade to black.)

ACT I
Scene Three

(A week later. Daytime. Joe is working on a computer with energy and enthusiasm. Nancy comes in with a cup of tea that she puts down on the table for him. He rises to grab hold of her. They kiss passionately, then finally break.)

NANCY. You should be working.

JOE. I am.

NANCY. You *should* be.

JOE. Are you pushing me away from you, Nancy?

NANCY. I would never do that. I'm just pushing you towards something else.

JOE. How many days has it been? Three? Four?

NANCY. It's been a week.

JOE. You can't be serious.

NANCY. I'm rarely anything else.

JOE. A week?

NANCY. This is the seventh day.

JOE. Time really has flown.

NANCY. Or absolutely stood still.

JOE. Yes. It's amazing how they both have the same effect, isn't it?

NANCY. Your writing seems to be going better.

JOE. I'm inspired. You inspire me.

NANCY. Good.

JOE. Good? It's great. It's a godsend.

NANCY. That's why I'm here.

JOE. *(with relish)* Roaring Gap.

NANCY. What about it?

JOE. That's where I'm setting the new story. It's going to be great. I can see it on my mind's movie screen as clearly as I do my boyhood village.

NANCY. But Roaring Gap is *not* your boyhood village.

JOE. So what?

NANCY. So why Roaring Gap?

JOE. It's near here.

NANCY. Yes, I know.

JOE. It's a great name. For a place. In which to set this story.

NANCY. No better a name than Panajachel.

JOE. What?

NANCY. Or Chichicastenango. Or San Antonio Aguas Calientes.

JOE. Nancy.

NANCY. Hmmmm?

JOE. What's your point?

NANCY. My point is that you're writing about worlds that are not your natural habitat.

JOE. North Carolina is where I *am*.

NANCY. Guatemala is where you're *from*.

JOE. Are you trying to pick a fight with me?

NANCY. No. I'm only trying to save your soul.

JOE. My body isn't enough? *(He laughs.)*

NANCY. No. *(She doesn't.)*

(He stops writing and turns to really look at her. She matches his look.)

JOE. What are you driving at?

NANCY. You're assimilated into a culture that is not truly your own. And not only have you done that by choice. It's your *preference*.

JOE. I don't deny my heritage.

NANCY. Don't you, Jose?

JOE. Joe.

(She raises an eyebrow to him as if to say, I rest my case. He realizes what he's just said, and tries to regroup.)

JOE. Look. Just because I'm open-minded enough to layer onto my inner core some surface characteristics of my adopted culture, does that mean I've abandoned my native heritage?

NANCY. Yes.

JOE. I beg your pardon?

NANCY. You should beg your own.

JOE. Name one way in which I've —

NANCY. Your books.

JOE. What?

NANCY. You heard me.

JOE. But you said —

NANCY. I said I was your most devout student. I never said I was your biggest fan.

JOE. I thought you liked my books.

NANCY. They're well-written. Deft. Entertaining. But they're also inauthentic.

JOE. Millions of people love them.

NANCY. Millions of people watch professional wrestling.

JOE. You're not saying...

NANCY. I'm not saying anything you don't already know in your assimilated little heart.

JOE. You're questioning how I write my stories? Why I choose the ones I do? Are you doubting my passion? My integrity?

NANCY. Only what you say, and how you say it.

(He rises. She sits comfortably and listens carefully.)

JOE. Language was my first love. My grand passion. The mistress of my heart and soul. Above all, I adored words. How they resonated so differently — the taste and feel of each individual word was a source of wonder to me. I devoured them, and they in turn consumed me. I became a man made of words — as much as I was flesh and blood, I was syllable and sound. I marveled at how "thigh" was so sensual a word, yet "hip" never aroused the blood. Why "anger" seemed so flat while "rage" ripped itself off the printed page. What the difference really was between "ominous" and "minatory." "Felicitous" smirked back at me from the page, while "perky" stayed obnoxious. Each word had its own personality, a look, a sound; left an echo in my mind and an image in my sight. Just to read the word "passion" could quicken my pulse; "thrilling" slithered into my ear and altered my breathing patterns. The word "groan" was somehow dispiriting; but whenever a woman "moaned," I could feel it climb down my spine and settle under my skin. The words we choose to use make us who we are, what each of us longs to be. When we read words on the page, the ones that move us show us our souls. When we tell our stories, the words we select define the tone, the tenor, the heartbeat of that story. And we are all of us, finally, the stories we tell.

NANCY. In your stories, you betray yourself.

JOE. No. I betray your picture of me.

NANCY. Jose can tell stories just as well as Joe.

JOE. Not better ones.

NANCY. Truer ones.

JOE. Different ones. When Jose is Joe, then Joe's story *is* the truth. *(beat)* What do *you* care, Nancy? Who are *you* to tell *me* I am not Latino enough? I mean, just who *are* you, anyway?

NANCY. You were born in your village for a reason. To be what you were meant to be.

JOE. What I am, is what I was meant to be. *(beat)* Who is it you have been making such glorious love with this past week? Joe or Jose?

NANCY. And who have *you* been with?

JOE. A stranger. A wild woman who never answers any question about herself but who tells me things about myself that I've long forgotten.

NANCY. And does that disturb you?

JOE. It makes me wonder; but then, I wonder as a way of life. So yes, I question it, but that does not mean I require an answer. I am not my father. I don't need to be sure I'm always right even when I'm being cruel or destructive. I don't have to always make a choice.

NANCY. And you think that being a detached observer of life makes you true to yourself?

JOE. Well. Yes.

NANCY. For all his faults — and they were legion — there was nothing fake about your father. He never pretended he was something he wasn't. So you're saying you're not the man your father was?

JOE. I want to be the man my father wasn't.

(She rises from the chair and, during the following, moves around the room sinuously, in a way that seems naturally, effortlessly mesmerizing.)

NANCY. You think you're so removed from him?

JOE. I'm as far away from him, his slashing belt, his child-molesting sicko brother, and that poverty-stricken shack, as I can get.

NANCY. Your father and his father — and his — demanded that the woman submit to the man. During sex.

JOE. Well, that's natural enough.

NANCY. You like being passive, Joe. Having me take charge.

JOE. Only because I want you to.

NANCY. So you think I'm still doing what you want?

JOE. Aren't you?

NANCY. I'm doing what you like. There's a difference.

JOE. Not to me.

NANCY. Joe. Get on your knees.

JOE. What?

NANCY. Kneel before me. I did it for you.

JOE. That was different.

NANCY. Was it?

JOE. It was to me.

NANCY. If you allow a woman to worship you, don't you think you should worship her as well?

JOE. Well. There are certain things…

NANCY. Exactly.

JOE. A man must always keep his dignity. Even when he is being most intimate with a woman. Especially then.

NANCY. That is a point of view. Your father's, in fact.

JOE. A woman who really cares about a man would never ask him to do… anything that made him uncomfortable. Would never *want* him to. She would want his dignity to remain unchallenged. Intact.

NANCY. At the cost of her own pleasure?

JOE. That would *be* her pleasure.

NANCY. As defined by you.

JOE. That is how *she* would define it.

NANCY. Only when you're wearing your father's shoes, Jose.

JOE. *(beat)* What do you want from me?

NANCY. I want you to do better work than you're doing. To reach not for success but for the raw expression of your naked dreams, whether or not critics cheer or audiences care. Tell the stories you have curled up in fetal positions, not those that skip cleverly across your mind. I want your spirit to dance in reckless abandon with the tormented shadows of your soul. To do what is right and beautiful and just, and not give a flying fuck whether anyone else in the world thinks it's immoral or evil or a disgrace to their notion of virtue.

JOE. Why is what I do so important to you?

NANCY. Because I love you, Joe. Don't you know that?

JOE. Yes. I do know that.

NANCY. Though you cannot imagine how much.

JOE. Yes. I can.

NANCY. No. You can't.

JOE. Nancy. Come here. Please.

NANCY. Jose would never have said please.

JOE. Screw that. Just come here.

(She does. He kisses her gently, passionately. She responds in kind. They break.)

JOE. Sit down. *(She does.)* Look. I didn't invite you here so that you could try to change me.

NANCY. You didn't invite me here at all.

JOE. Well, in a sense I did.

NANCY. You're hallucinating, Joe.

JOE. That's sort of what I'm trying to tell you. *(beat)* Nancy, do you think much about the nature of reality?

NANCY. No.

JOE. Only on occasion?

NANCY. Never.

JOE. Not at all?

NANCY. No. It's a total waste of time. It's like trying to teach a pig to sing. All you ever succeed in doing is to frustrate yourself and annoy the pig.

JOE. I would have thought that you'd want to know.

NANCY. About the nature of reality?

JOE. Yes.

NANCY. I *do* know.

JOE. You do?

NANCY. Oh, yes. *(pause)*

JOE. Are you going to tell me?

NANCY. *(beat)* A tiger fell asleep in a tree one day, and dreamed that he *was* the tree. From then on, he was never completely certain he wasn't a tree, dreaming *it* was a *tiger*.

JOE. And you think that's the nature of reality?

NANCY. I *know* it is.

JOE. Nancy. Did it ever occur to you that I'm making you up?

NANCY. You mean that you don't know the real me?

JOE. No. I mean that I'm making you up. That you don't really exist unless I believe that you do.

NANCY. Things are simpler than you're making them.

JOE. It is possible that you're unreal. I've had all kinds of weird relationships with characters I've created.

NANCY. Like your imaginary buddy Luke who always beat up all those jerks from the Barbera gang in your imagination, when you were eight.

JOE. Yes, like that. You couldn't possibly know about Luke unless I'm projecting you into this room. I mean, no one ever knew about Luke. I never even said his name. To anyone.

NANCY. Except to Joanne when you told her *everything* during all that perfect sex.

JOE. There you go again. Joanne was totally an imagined movie star I just conjured off the screen. I only ever saw her when I closed my eyes in bed at night, that's why the sex was always so perfect. I mean why do you suppose I mostly prefer imagination to reality?

NANCY. I *know* why.

JOE. I know you know. That's why I figure you're not real. That is, you are, but only to you and me.

NANCY. Who else matters?

JOE. It doesn't mean I desire you any less. And just because you may not be real, doesn't mean you're not a fine person.

NANCY. You really think I don't exist?

JOE. It's just a possibility. Maybe you really *are* this weird and wonderful woman whose whole life seems to be devoted to mine. But then, if that *is* who you are, then in a sense I'm making you up anyway, aren't I?

NANCY. You don't know how ironic this is.

JOE. Well, no, I don't. If it is. Is it?

NANCY. Oh, yes.

JOE. Are you suggesting that you're *not* my creation?

NANCY. Oh, Joe. You sweet, stupid, self-absorbed little boy.

JOE. Watch it.

NANCY. I *am* watching it. You know, for someone who's become famous for understanding things, you really don't have a clue, do you?

JOE. I think it's time we established once and for all who's in charge around here.

NANCY. I quite agree.

JOE. I'm the man. You're the woman. I'm the leader. You're the follower. I'm the star. You're the astronomer.

NANCY. You're the personification of ignorance. I'm the source of knowledge. You're the empty computer mainframe. I'm the chip with all the information. You're the man. I am... who I am. How's your tea?

JOE. My tea? My tea is perfect. Thanks.

NANCY. You're welcome. Has it been anything but perfect all week?

JOE. No. Why?

NANCY. Has *anything* been less than perfect all week? The sex? The constellations in the nighttime sky? The vermicelli primavera?

JOE. Everything has been flawless. And that was the best pasta I've ever had.

NANCY. So everything has been ideal.

JOE. Totally.

NANCY. And your explanation for this is to decide that you've made me up?

JOE. It's not meant as a criticism.

NANCY. Joe. You've got it backwards.

JOE. I don't understand.

NANCY. You never did.

JOE. What are you saying?

NANCY. You didn't create me.

JOE. You can't be sure of that.

NANCY. Oh, yes I can.

JOE. How can you?

NANCY. Because *I* created *you*.

JOE. You're crazy.

NANCY. No. I'm not. I'm... well...

JOE. You're what?

NANCY. I'm... God.

(Pause. Then he laughs uproariously. She doesn't. He stops, and is silent. So is she.)

JOE. Excuse me?

NANCY. I always have.

JOE. Don't be ridiculous.

NANCY. I never am.

JOE. Do you expect me to take this seriously?

NANCY. Not really. For a writer, your imagination is distressingly limited.

JOE. I'm supposed to believe that God is a woman named Nancy?

NANCY. Surely you believe that God can take any form at all. Why not a woman called Nancy? Does that make any less sense than a man named Jesus?

JOE. I'll bet a lot of people think they're God.

NANCY. More than you imagine.

JOE. So what makes you different?

NANCY. Everything.

(Pause. They regard each other. He's amused, skeptical, terrified. She's serene.)

JOE. I'm going to need proof.

NANCY. Oh, ye of little faith.

JOE. What do you expect?

NANCY. You would never understand the answer to that. How *could* you, really? Okay. Cheap tricks it is. You ready?

JOE. For what?

NANCY. Showtime.

JOE. Born ready.

NANCY. If you say so. Now, don't panic, Joe. You can no longer speak. You can't make a sound.

(He tries, but can't. He is momentarily panic-stricken.)

NANCY. All right. You can speak normally again.

(He tries, and can. He checks himself out, looks at her with increasing fear.)

JOE. That's pretty good. But that could have been...

NANCY. All right. Let's do another. You're blind.

(He is. He breathes rapidly, panic-stricken, as he stumbles and gropes around)

JOE. What?... How?...

NANCY. But now can see.

(He can. Again. He looks at her with growing awe, but there's still that shadow of a doubt. She smiles with understanding, almost affection.)

NANCY. You're right. They *are* tricks, really. Okay, Joe. I'll let you see the ace in the hole, so that we can move on to the business at hand.

(She rises, and her presence becomes palpably more commanding and majestic. She speaks with quiet authority.)

NANCY. Behold, Joe. Behold.

(Joe is struck by a vision that leaves him overwhelmed, transformed. There are no effects of any kind visible to us; his awed rapture is entirely internal.)

JOE. Oh... my... God.

NANCY. Yes.

JOE. Yes.

NANCY. Yes.

(He sinks to his knees at her feet, as if to worship her. She stops him by reaching down and drawing him to her. Still on his knees, he buries his head in her stomach and clutches her tightly in an embrace as if he will never let go. She lets him do so, and, with infinite gentleness, strokes his head. They stay like that as the lights fade. END OF ACT I)

ACT II
Scene One

(Joe and Nancy are engaged in sexual grappling. During the following exchange, they constantly change positions. First one is dominant and the other conquered or submissive, then it shifts quickly and suddenly, then again, and so on throughout.)

JOE. I don't know.

NANCY. Well, of course not.

JOE. How can I believe in you?

NANCY. How can you not?

JOE. How long will you stay with me?

NANCY. I'm always with you.

JOE. Shouldn't you be with other people as well?

NANCY. What makes you think I'm not?

JOE. But you're here now.

NANCY. I'm *there* now, too.

JOE. Where?

NANCY. With everyone.

JOE. You mean...

NANCY. Of course.

JOE. This is all just... too much.

NANCY. Of course it's too much. You think you can fuck with divinity and not be overwhelmed by the experience?

JOE. I *am* overwhelmed.

NANCY. And you're not accustomed to that, are you?

JOE. No. And the thought has occurred to me.

NANCY. Ah.

JOE. Well, it's just that… I was thinking…

NANCY. Yes?

JOE. You could be the Devil. Couldn't you?

(Nancy suddenly separates herself from him and creates a certain distance. Still, the sexual tension, and mutual palpable desire, doesn't abate at all.)

NANCY. I was wondering when you'd get to that.

JOE. I mean, this *is* the way the Devil would tempt me.

NANCY. Like you'd know.

JOE. Well, isn't it?

NANCY. Actually, no. She's far likelier to invest you with a sense of pious morality that you feel obligated to go around imposing on everyone else. That's what she usually likes to do. Righteousness is her standard M.O. Haven't you noticed that?

JOE. I've noticed that *you* never seem to be quite what you seem.

NANCY. Do you really think I'm her?

JOE. You *could* be, couldn't you? For a week, everything's been unrealistically perfect, you've been the greatest dream lover imaginable, and you haven't answered a single one of my questions about why, if you *are* God, terrible things keep happening to the innocent.

NANCY. "Unrealistic." I love that word. And "innocent." Yes, well.

JOE. So what am I supposed to…

NANCY. Faith.

JOE. That's your answer?

NANCY. Have you got a better one?

JOE. I'm a little uncomfortable with this whole situation, to tell you the truth.

NANCY. It's not a situation that lends itself to comfort, is it?

JOE. I mean having... carnal relations with you. It's kind of late to worry about it now, I know. But you have to admit it *could* be considered... well... a little...

NANCY. A little what?

JOE. Perverse. Blasphemous.

NANCY. Does it feel that way to you?

JOE. Well, *shouldn't* it bother me? How could it *not*?

NANCY. Do you enjoy sex, Joe?

JOE. Like you don't know.

NANCY. But do you love it? With inspired passion?

JOE. Of course. You know that as well as I do.

NANCY. Better.

JOE. So?

NANCY. So whose invention do you think *that* is?

JOE. Are you telling me that carnality is sanctified?

NANCY. Ding-ding-ding!

JOE. But how can...

NANCY. Come on, I know you've considered the question. You've even written about it, though not nearly as well as you're going to now. Think about it. Since I created you with the overwhelming sex drive you naturally have, then how on earth could you possibly think sex is anything but holy? Sexual passion is a sacred trust. Deny it at the peril of your immortal soul.

JOE. Is my soul really immortal?

NANCY. Rhetorically speaking.

JOE. Nancy, we've been knocking it off like two teenagers in heat rolling around in the back seat of a Chevy. Are you really telling me that's as holy as going to church?

NANCY. It *is* church. I'm talking pure, unadulterated, mutual passion. Nothing less. You have a problem with that?

JOE. Just the occasional guilt.

NANCY. Speak of the Devil. Guilt is little Lucy's invention, not mine, and it's a damned clever one. It's so typical of her to lay that on all of you, then credit it to me. Personally, I don't believe in guilt.

JOE. Then what *do* you believe in?

NANCY. Truth and consequences.

JOE. I'm a fan of the first.

NANCY. Can't you just adore me with unconditional love?

JOE. If only it were that simple.

NANCY. It *is* that simple. It just isn't that easy.

JOE. But you still *could* be the Devil. Couldn't you?

NANCY. Of course I could. That's her basic technique, after all. To seem like me. She's such a jealous bitch. Not that I don't understand her envy.

JOE. But you're saying she can't be like you.

NANCY. Of course she can. She looks just like me. The difference is, she doesn't love you.

JOE. But if she looks like you, and came to me as you did, and told me she was the dream my dreams dream of…

NANCY. You wouldn't be able to tell the difference. You can't *now*, can you? You're wondering even as you look at me. But it doesn't make you desire me any less, does it?

JOE. Well. No.

NANCY. And that's why she's trouble. You wouldn't have a chance with her.

JOE. Do I have a chance with *you*?

NANCY. Always.

JOE. Really?

NANCY. Take your chance, Joe. Take me. And be taken *by* me.

JOE. It's tempting. But it's also scary.

NANCY. Yes, it is. But you should be more scared about *not* taking the chance. That should be a truly terrifying prospect.

JOE. Why?

NANCY. Because you're dust. You are not impressive in your original form. Not a lot of sublime ecstasy in being a handful of dust. You've been given a great enormous gift. To not take it while you can would be... ungrateful.

JOE. Nancy. If you're God. You could *make* me believe. Anything. Couldn't you?

NANCY. Free will, baby. That's the nature of the process. That's the whole point, though I wouldn't expect you to understand that. No one has, really, except Einstein, and he never understood that that was *what* he had understood.

JOE. Free will.

NANCY. I know your thoughts. But I don't control them. That would be like pre-determining which bat hits which pitch.

JOE. You're a baseball fan?

NANCY. My favorite game. There's no clock in baseball, have you ever thought about that? It's truly timeless. In theory, if you just kept getting hits and never made three outs, you could go on playing forever. The inning would never end. I find that pursuit of immortality rather charming, don't you? But I would never want to know the final score in advance. That would take all the sweet pleasure out of discovering, pitch by brave pitch, the unexpected struggles of that particular game. Kiss me.

JOE. Again?

NANCY. Of course, again. Kisses feed upon themselves. The more of them you have, the more you want. Neither capacity nor desire is meant to diminish. That was the whole point of inventing kisses.

JOE. But if you're the devil…

NANCY. Then you're already damned. I wouldn't worry about it. You won't know in this lifetime anyway. So just do the best you can. Which is me.

(Joe and Nancy kiss. Passionately. Then he pulls away.)

JOE. Faith?

NANCY. Absolutely.

JOE. And if I doubt…

NANCY. Get over it.

JOE. Nancy.

(She moves sinuously around and against him. She is mesmerizing him into an instinctive, primitive dance.)

NANCY. Lose yourself in me.

JOE. Then I'll be lost.

NANCY. Quite the opposite. That's the only way you will ever be found.

JOE. I need to find out, not to be found.

(Nancy kisses him. He yields and responds. They come up for air.)

JOE. This can't be right.

NANCY. Why? Because it feels too good?

JOE. I don't want to feel… ashamed.

NANCY. Ashamed of what? Of your body? Of mine? Of how they fit together? What they want to do, is what they were made to do. Honor their creator. Shame is for those who follow the serpent instead of me. Shame is the blanket Little Lucy gives you, to protect you from a wind that isn't really blowing. If you wrap yourself in shame, you're keeping my warmth out, not in.

(They embrace again. He pulls away uneasily again.)

JOE. I'm afraid, Nancy.

NANCY. Of being in my embrace?

JOE. Yes.

NANCY. Be afraid of *not* being in it.

JOE. I am. I'm terrified of both, I guess.

NANCY. Joe. Am I not what you always wanted?

JOE. Yes.

NANCY. What you always longed for? Even prayed for?

JOE. Yes.

NANCY. Then why do you deny me?

JOE. Because I can't be sure.

NANCY. That's right. You can't. Not ever.

JOE. Then whatever I do…

NANCY. May be heaven or hell, salvation or damnation. So why not just do it, instead of trying to understand what you will never know? Why deny pleasure because someone's trying to make you feel guilty for feeling it? Why hesitate at buying into bliss, just because someone's trying to sell you shame?

JOE. Why do I feel as though I'm standing at the edge of an abyss?

NANCY. Because you are. You were *born* on one. Some day you will fall into it. So dance while you can.

(They move in harmony with each other.)

JOE. Nancy.

NANCY. Yes.

JOE. I believe you. That you're not the devil.

NANCY. Do you? Truly?

JOE. I think so, yes.

NANCY. But do you believe *in* me?

JOE. Well…

NANCY. I see.

JOE. All your knowledge. The things you did to me. They could be illusions. Couldn't they?

NANCY. What about the vision I let you see?

JOE. I don't pretend to know how you did it.

NANCY. But you think maybe there's a trick to it.

JOE. It could be magic.

NANCY. Of course.

JOE. Or you could still be a figment of my imagination.

NANCY. Or you of mine.

JOE. Can I still worship you even if you *aren't* God?

NANCY. If you worship me, who else *am* I?

JOE. What do you want from me?

NANCY. Only your body and your soul.

JOE. *(sardonic)* That's all?

NANCY. It does sound like a lot, doesn't it?

JOE. Are you going to tell me it isn't?

NANCY. Of course not. But haven't you spent your entire life looking for and fantasizing about a woman you loved enough to give yourself to completely?

JOE. Yes.

NANCY. Your fondest desire has been realized. The question is, why are you hesitating to accept it?

JOE. Because I have the feeling you want something more from me.

NANCY. I do.

JOE. Are you going to tell me? Or is there a passage of scripture somewhere that I need to interpret?

NANCY. You could say that. Only it hasn't been written yet.

JOE. How do you mean?

NANCY. I want your book. The one you were created to write.

JOE. How do I know which one that is?

NANCY. *I* know. I'll tell you, when you've written it.

JOE. I wouldn't want you to be disappointed.

NANCY. No, you really wouldn't.

JOE. I've got to write what I feel. The way I feel it. You do know that.

NANCY. Just complete the novel.

JOE. I shouldn't worry about the reviews?

NANCY. There will only be one that matters.

JOE. All right. I'll write the book.

NANCY. Of course you will.

JOE. And afterwards...

NANCY. Never concern yourself with afterwards. Never. Never. Never. Never. Never.

(She kisses him gently, eternally. He responds. Lights fade to black as scene ends.)

ACT II
Scene Two

(Joe is writing. It's obviously become intense and difficult for him. He labors. Nancy enters.)

NANCY. How's it going?

JOE. To tell you the truth, I have no idea.

NANCY. Sounds promising.

(He offers her some pages. She takes them, sits, makes herself comfortable, and reads. He keeps working, but glances at her to catch any reaction.)

NANCY. "Aerodynamically, bees can't fly. The way they're built, it's scientifically impossible. But it seems that nobody told the bees."

JOE. Too much, do you think?

NANCY. Depends on the context, doesn't it?

JOE. Want to read some more?

NANCY. I'll wait until it's finished.

JOE. And then?

NANCY. Then I'll read it all. Every syllable.

JOE. And pass judgment.

NANCY. Yes.

(He stops writing. They regard each other.)

JOE. You know, I've been thinking about that. Your passing judgment on me. And how one reader's masterpiece can be another reader's piece of junk. Yet they're the same book. The same words on the same page. The difference in experience isn't the writer. It's the reader.

NANCY. And your point is?

JOE. That both the writer and the reader are totally dependent on each other. Each one needs the other.

NANCY. So?

JOE. So I've been wondering.

NANCY. Yes?

JOE. I'm still trying to figure out if I was made in your image, or you were made in mine.

NANCY. You still think there's a difference?

JOE. It's just that if you *are* God... If you really created me...

NANCY. Yes?

JOE. Then I created you, too. *(beat)* After all, if you're my God, here to protect me, looking out for me, then you're only here because I believe in you.

NANCY. I wish you wouldn't do this.

ACT II • SCENE TWO

JOE. You only even exist because I think you do. If I wasn't willing to buy into you... well... I did invent you too, didn't I, Nancy? Just as much as you created me. *(beat)* Unless you *are* just a crazy bitch who's done a hell of a job researching me.

NANCY. Jose.

JOE. Call me Joe. Free will, right?

NANCY. Joe. Don't question me.

JOE. I'm questioning you. Nancy.

NANCY. I *am* your God.

JOE. Then behave like one. Do what *I* want.

NANCY. I *am* doing what you want. You just have no idea what it really *is* you want, and I can't explain it to you, and I wouldn't even if I could. That's part of the deal.

JOE. If I stop believing in you, you'll go away, won't you?

NANCY. Well...

JOE. You'd have to. Wouldn't you?

NANCY. You are nothing without me. Less than nothing.

JOE. You need me as much as I need you. More, maybe.

NANCY. Of course I need you, you idiot. If I didn't need you, why on earth would I have created you? You think you're more impressive than oceans, or more admirable than a panther? You're my grand experiment, Joe — the answer to the question, how far should I go? Why would I have created evolution if I hadn't desired to be speaking with you here and now? Of course I need you. I'm alone. Did you ever think about that? How completely lonely it is to be this *only*? I demand your attention because I *need* your attention. Don't you think I *deserve* to be recognized for what I am? Don't you feel that I *should* be worshipped by those thoughtful enough to realize all I've done? Those I have, after all, *created*? Given *life*?

JOE. I'm losing faith in you, Nancy.

NANCY. Don't.

JOE. You need me to imagine you.

NANCY. You need me to create you.

JOE. You need me to believe in you.

NANCY. Listen. You ever hear of the wrath of God? You don't want to know about it.

JOE. Damnation?

NANCY. More or less.

JOE. But who's damning whom?

NANCY. I'm the deity. You're the mortal subject. It's a one-way, dead-end street. Make no mistake about who's got the power here.

JOE. But where do you get it *from*? Who's *giving* it to you?

NANCY. I can kill you, remember.

JOE. I know. But what'll happen to *you*, if you do?

NANCY. Are you really prepared to find out?

JOE. Why not?

NANCY. Because you're an artist, Joe. You've chosen a creative existence.

JOE. So?

NANCY. So you need to express yourself. You can't do that nearly as well if you're dead. And you have potential, Joe. You're good, but you want to be great. I can help you do that. Death can't. Trust me on this one.

JOE. You're too hard to trust, Nancy.

NANCY. Then don't trust me. Just believe in me.

JOE. You're a little too divine for me to believe in.

NANCY. Touch me. Feel me. I'm flesh and blood.

JOE. Yeah, but whose?

NANCY. I'm all you've got.

JOE. But what if you lose me?

NANCY. You're a speck of dust.

JOE. But I'm *your* speck of dust. If I reject you, where does that leave *you*?

NANCY. Right where I am.

JOE. Without me.

NANCY. That's not the loss you think it is.

JOE. Then why are you here, Nancy? Why are you with me, unless you *need* to be with me?

NANCY. I told you. I showed you. I made you *feel* why.

JOE. You made me want you. But wanting isn't enough.

NANCY. Nothing is ever enough to a human who wants more. Why do you write, Joe?

JOE. Because I want to.

NANCY. And?

JOE. Because I need to.

NANCY. And?

JOE. Because I have to.

NANCY. Because you want to say something?

JOE. Because I have something to say.

NANCY. Exactly. So finish your book.

JOE. Why is this one so —

NANCY. Just write it.

JOE. You never visited me before.

NANCY. You never *saw* me before.

JOE. I mean to help me with the other books.

NANCY. I'm here now.

JOE. That's just what I'm wondering. Why now?

NANCY. Because you need me now.

JOE. You're not going to tell me, are you?

NANCY. I'm going to show you.

JOE. You are?

NANCY. Oh, yes.

JOE. Promise?

NANCY. Yes. Afterwards.

JOE. Afterwards?

NANCY. Take my hand, Joe. *(beat)* Go on. Touch it. It won't be the first time, will it?

(After a moment, he does. She displays her hand to him in different ways.)

NANCY. Do you think much about the human hand? All the things it can do. It can feel. Grasp. Ecstasy can be transmitted through these fingers. Feel my touch on your cheek, there. Nothing quite like it, is there? The pleasure a gentle, well-placed touch can give is as great to the one touching, as to the one being touched. Have you considered how amazing that is? And as you know, it can also be a weapon, even a deadly one. When Cain struck down Abel, he didn't really understand what he'd done, but he *felt* it. Felt it right down to the nerve ends that rested beneath his fingernails. This hand can build a fortress, coax sublime music from a silent keyboard, deliver a child… bury a friend. It can form characters that become words on a page, and those words become images in someone's mind, and those images become thoughts, visions, revelations, and those revelations change the reality in which the reader lives. You have a mighty power, Joe. I've given you that power. If you accept that gift — and you have — you accept with it the obligation to use that gift not wisely, but well. And you cannot use it well enough if you ever lose sight of the miracle itself— that hand you carry so carelessly, and all it can do. If you cease to marvel at what you've been given, Joe, you will cease to fully appreciate the glory of the brief, brutal, shining, passing moment in which I have allowed you to exist. If you ever take that hand for granted, then you take *me* for granted. And that is something you should never, ever do.

JOE. Nancy. If I closed my eyes — would you still be there?

NANCY. Of course.

JOE. And if I closed my mind and my heart? If I shut all the doors to my soul and threw away the keys? Where would you be then, Nancy?

(They stand still, facing each other.)

JOE. Would you *be*?

(They continue to regard each other as the lights fade, and the scene ends.)

ACT II
Scene Three

(Nancy is sitting in the chair, reading a thick manuscript. She is almost at the end of it. Joe paces nervously around the room, adjusting things that don't need adjusting, busying himself with mindless and irrelevant tasks as he waits for her to finish.)

JOE. Taking you a long time for an all-knowing deity.

NANCY. When I'm in human form, I'm on your pace. I'll admit it's an adjustment, but it has its pleasures. Don't you *want* your book to be read slowly and carefully?

JOE. I want appreciation and praise.

NANCY. I know the feeling.

JOE. Am I bothering you by talking?

NANCY. Not at all. I am the personification of multi-tasking.

JOE. Not me. When I'm writing, I don't even think about eating, drinking, or talking to anyone else. I wouldn't hear a bomb if it went off in my ear. All I can think about is the next word I need to put down on paper.

NANCY. So long as the next word is the best one you could have chosen.

JOE. I started writing because I needed a way to express everything I was feeling. I passed people on the street and made up their life stories to entertain myself. I saw a middle-aged couple and pictured their children who would become, let's see: the girl, a cynical doctor, the boy, an optimistic serial killer. A man in a raincoat looking into a store window became a lawyer who dreamed of being a figure skater. A fortyish woman in a green hat was going home to assault her daughter. But her daughter's boyfriend was building bombs in his basement because he needed a political excuse for his need to destroy. Everyone I passed had a story that I made up for them. The reality of these people did not interest me. Only the truth of what I saw in them. I needed to write these stories. I wanted to... to...

NANCY. To play God.

JOE. I suppose you could put it that way.

NANCY. Only you aren't a god. You're just another human desperate to make a difference. To do something, anything, that might actually matter.

JOE. Not "anything." It had to be writing.

NANCY. Ah. Yes.

JO. Writing for as many people as possible who would understand what I was trying to say. Even if that audience was only one reader I'd never met. Searching for someone, anyone, who would *get* it; who would see with my eyes, feel with my fingers, dance to the blood that beat through my restless heart. Reaching, now and forever, for The Unknown Friend.

NANCY. Without ever knowing whether you actually touched them.

JOE. Damn it, Nancy. If you made me, then you made me this way. What do you want from me?

NANCY. The absolute best of which you're capable. And nothing less.

JOE. I'm trying.

NANCY. Trying's not enough. Not any more.

JOE. Why? What's changed?

NANCY. Everything. Nothing.

JOE. That's a bit enigmatic.

NANCY. What do you expect from God? An explanation?

JOE. Just tell me what *has* changed.

NANCY. You, Joe. You've changed.

JO. How?

NANCY. The book.

JOE. The one you're reading?

NANCY. I've read it.

JOE. You finished it?

NANCY. Yes.

JOE. When?

NANCY. Now.

JOE. You were going to tell me. When you finished it.

NANCY. I *am* telling you.

JOE. And? Are you surprised? Disappointed? Angry?

NANCY. I'm pleased.

JOE. You are?

NANCY. Oh, yes.

JOE. But it's not what you wanted.

NANCY. Do you really think you have any comprehension of what *I* wanted?

JOE. You *told* me.

NANCY. What did you hear me tell you?

JOE. To write about Guatemala. And I didn't, did I?

NANCY. I wanted you to write as though you were *from* Guatemala. Because you are. And now you have.

JOE. You wanted me to write about Chichicastenango.

NANCY. Someone who grows up in Chichicastenango and never goes anywhere else can write about life in Chichicastenango. Someone who never leaves Roaring Gap can write about Roaring Gap. But only someone who has lived in both can tell us what the differences mean.

JOE. I thought...

NANCY. You thought what I meant by authentic was for you to write as though you were still in your boyhood village. But you're not in that village, Jose. You haven't been for a long time. Don't you think I know that?

JOE. Then what was all that about authenticity?

NANCY. Authentic means who you really are. Not who you once were, long ago.

JOE. What's different in this book from what I would have written anyway?

NANCY. Joe, do you believe that everything that happens to you has an effect on who you are? That you become a subtly different version of yourself with the impact of every major incident in your life?

JOE. Sure.

NANCY. And do I qualify as a major incident?

JOE. They don't come any more major than you, Nancy.

NANCY. Then my... visitation, has had an effect on you, yes? The way you regard the universe, and see your world?

JOE. Of course.

NANCY. This book. This story. Could only have been written by the man you are. Not Jose, whom you thought I wanted. And not Joe, whom you thought *you* wanted. But the Jose who has become Joe.

JOE. And that's what you wanted?

NANCY. That's what I wanted.

JOE Why?

NANCY. I didn't want a book that was good, clever, even brilliant. I wanted the book that no one could have written but you.

JOE. And this is it?

NANCY. Don't you think it is?

JOE. All the other books I've written — I was proud of them at the time. They were good, I thought, for what they were. Dramatic, suspenseful, and if you're going to comment on politics and social values, there's nothing wrong with being entertaining. Why should anyone read or watch anything if it isn't entertaining? Yes, they were genre — suspense, thriller, drama, whatever they were — but so what? *The Brothers Karamazov* is a whodunit. What's wrong with genre? But it's true, I haven't ever put myself fully and deeply into them, not the way I did in this one. I've never written events that I have truly experienced as I have these — though little in this book actually happened.

NANCY. That's okay. I never let facts interfere with truth, either.

JOE. If there is such a thing as a book I was born to write — a story no one else would have told in exactly this way — I think this is probably as close as I'm going to get to it.

NANCY. This *is* as close as you're going to get to it.

JOE. You don't think I can do even better?

NANCY. It's not a question of better.

JOE. Well, then, explore my uniqueness in an even richer way. You know, improve on it in some fashion. Or at least develop the themes a bit further. Take the journey a few steps farther down the road. Do you know what I'm asking?

NANCY. Of course.

JOE. So don't you think that's possible? At least hypothetically?

NANCY. No.

JOE. No?

NANCY. No.

JOE. Why not?

NANCY. *(infinitely gentle)* You know why not.

JOE. *(beat)* Oh. No.

NANCY. I'm afraid so.

JOE. But...

NANCY. Whatever you're about to say, Joe, it's all been said before, more times than you could possibly imagine. It's never made the slightest difference, and it never will. It's not about logic or reason or circumstance or words or gestures. It's not about anything at all. That's the point.

JOE. But I've just hit my stride. Found my truest voice.

NANCY. Then you should be grateful for that, shouldn't you?

JOE. But... *Now?*

NANCY. That's life. It always ends.

JOE. "That's life?" Is that really the best you can do?

NANCY. Well. No. But I don't need to impress you, do I?

JOE. Look. I wouldn't tell anyone about you.

NANCY. What difference would it make if you did? No one would believe you, except people who read supermarket magazines. Anyone else would figure you're delusional, or they'd take it as a metaphor. People take almost everything as a metaphor. Not that almost everything isn't. You'd be lucky if you weren't locked up. This isn't about telling people, Joe. This is about existence being finite.

JOE. But the book...

NANCY. Don't worry about its future. If you and I like it, no one else matters.

JOE. My friends...

NANCY. And family, and admirers, will all be distressed for awhile. They were going to be, sooner or later, anyway. What did you *think* was going to happen, Joe?

JOE. Would you have come for me — I mean, now — if it wasn't for the book?

NANCY. I come for everyone, Joe. In one form or another. Eventually.

JOE. But if I hadn't...

NANCY. If you hadn't written the book you were meant to write?

JOE. Yes.

NANCY. Then you would have come and gone without ever having done the best of which you were capable. But failure to fulfill yourself doesn't lengthen your stay. I don't give extensions — at least, not as a rule.

JOE. And I'm not the exception?

NANCY. Being exceptional doesn't mean you get an exception. Besides, you've already had one.

JOE. What do you mean?

NANCY. I let you complete your story.

JOE. You mean...

NANCY. Exactly.

JOE. *(beat)* I should have known.

NANCY. Well. You *were* a bit distracted.

JOE. No calls. No people. Nothing but you and me since you arrived. And now...

NANCY. Now you know.

JOE. *What* do I know?

NANCY. All you're ever *going* to know.

JOE. So if not for your... visit... I might have never written the book I just wrote.

NANCY. It's hard to see how you *could* have.

JOE. I suppose I should thank you.

NANCY. There's no need. It was my choice to do it this way.

JOE. Then for the visit.

NANCY. Everyone gets one. It's the last thing they see.

JOE. What happens now?

NANCY. To be determined.

JOE. The readiness is all.

NANCY. *Are* you ready?

JOE. Don't know. I don't think so.

NANCY. That's okay. Very few are.

JOE. Nancy? What was it all for?

NANCY. What do *you* think?

JOE. I don't know. I remember all the nights I stared at the sky and wondered what the heavens held that I could not imagine. It was an ironic thought, I realized later, because I was actually trying to imagine what it was that I could not imagine. I did understand the first time I ever saw them why the stars were considered romantic — they were so beautiful, inspiring, magical, and just plain perfect.

NANCY. Yes, they are. But so are snowflakes, and pineapples.

JOE. I'm remembering the oddest things.

NANCY. They're not odd. They're just not what you expected to remember in your final moments.

JOE. When I was sixteen. That summer night with Donna. Not the sex — amazing as that felt — but afterwards. Watching her just leaning back on the couch, wearing my blue work shirt that was so big on her, and nothing else. Just the way she looked, lying there, this sophisticated older woman who somehow, miraculously, wanted me.

NANCY. She was twenty.

JOE. With that long blond hair tumbling over her shoulders and chest like a golden waterfall.

NANCY. It wasn't natural. She was born brunette.

JOE. I didn't know. I didn't care.

NANCY. Nor should you have.

JOE. I looked at her and I thought, this is what it feels like to be happy. This is bliss.

NANCY. And so it was.

JOE. I never saw her again after that summer. Right now, I can't imagine why I ever left at all that night.

NANCY. Because the moment couldn't last forever. Nothing does.

JOE. Whatever happened to Donna? Where is she now? Does she remember me as I remember her?

NANCY. Does it matter?

JOE. Nancy. I'm scared.

NANCY. That's natural.

JOE. I'm terrified.

NANCY. You don't have to be.

JOE. Will everything be all right?

NANCY. Everything will be what it is. Regardless of how you feel about that.

JOE. So this is it? This is all there is?

NANCY. All.

JOE. Nothing else remains?

NANCY. Nothing.

JOE. I can't help wondering if I've done enough. If I've left enough behind. If what I've written will make any difference to anyone's life.

NANCY. It doesn't matter any more. It will or it won't.

JOE. Nancy.

NANCY. I know. You want words of comfort.

JOE. *Are* there any?

NANCY. In the beginning was the word.

JOE. And in the end?

(Nancy smiles at him, takes his hand, holds it. The stage is bathed in brilliant white light. Then all goes suddenly, abruptly black.)

END OF PLAY

Props

| A gun (does not need to fire) | A computer | Sheaf of pages |

The Baseball Game of the Week

by James McLure

Characters

DAZZY   BOOTER   MIKE   KIMBLE   HAVELMEYER   HOAGIE

Place: Announcer's booth. Radio. Cluttered desk. Microphones. Pads. Styrofoam cups. A day game between the Yankees and the Indians in Cleveland.

Time: The recent past... which in terms of baseball can mean many things.

ACT I

Lights fade.   "Take Me Out to the Ballgame" slowly played.

Then some VOICES from the past: MEL ALLEN, RED BARBER, HARRY CAREY, "DIZZY" DEAN, PHIL RIZZUTO...

"Gillette" theme song.
"Nice guys never finish first."
"The Giants win the pennant..." etc.
"Lou Gehrig's speech..."

Through the first ten pages the sound should slowly increase as the stadium fills with people. Afterwards modulate as needed to suit the play of the game and the dialogue.

OL' DAZ enters. He is a huge pot-bellied old redneck. He pops open a beer with a church key. He stands in the doorway with beer, hotdog. He eats the hotdog in three big, quick bites. He picks up the microphone and speaks in a bright cheery voice. BOOTER enters, stands in the doorway.

DAZZY. Howdy everyone. This is Ol' Daz, your colorful baseball announcer telling the whole civilized Western world to go fructurate itself.

(BOOTER enters. He is graying, forties, but still trim. Wears glasses.)

BOOTER. Hey, Daz.

DAZZY. Aw, hiya Booter.

BOOTER. Say Daz, was that mic on?

DAZZY. *(pause)* Naw.

BOOTER. Good. That's a good thing. Because you can't say things like that on the air.

DAZZY. Things like what?

BOOTER. Telling the world to go fructurate itself.

DAZZY. Why the hell not? Why can't I tell the world to go fructurate itself?

BOOTER. Because it's bad for baseball, Daz.

DAZZY. Aw, to hell with it.

BOOTER. It's bad for baseball and it's bad for the morals of the country.

DAZZY. Aw man —

BOOTER. And you know why else you can't do it, Daz? Why you can't tell the country to go fructurate itself?

DAZZY. Why?

BOOTER. Because of the kids, Daz. Think of the kids. Holy bovine. If the kids hear fructurate. Holy bovine.

DAZZY. *(pause)* You're right.

BOOTER. I know I'm right.

DAZZY. I will abstain from profanity.

BOOTER. Atta boy, Daz.

DAZZY. On the air.

BOOTER. Say — what does fructurate mean anyhow?

DAZZY. I think it means sex with a peach.

BOOTER. I don't object to salty language now and again as long as it's off the air. Holy bovine — I've been known to curse once in awhile myself. But my lovely bride, Connie, doesn't like it.

DAZZY. You're the only guy I know who's been married as long as you have —

BOOTER. We don't need to go into details on that one —

DAZZY. But you still refer to your wife as your lovely bride.

BOOTER. I'd refer to her as something else but — whoo, boy. I'd get the rolling pin for sure. *(An OMNISCIENT VOICE suddenly comes on.)*

MIKE. Booter?

BOOTER. Yeah.

MIKE. This is Mike.

BOOTER. Mike? Mike who?

MIKE. Mike in the control booth.

BOOTER. Oh! Right! That Mike! The Mike in the control booth. Right.

MIKE. Right.

BOOTER. Listen — are you still in control? Ha-ha-ha.

MIKE. Marginally —

BOOTER. Listen — sorry, it's my Alzheimer's. Ha-ha-ha.

MIKE. Listen, is Daz there? *(Daz burps. Titanically.)* Hi Daz. Good burp. Since this is your last — I wanna say something sentimental but since I'm not a sentimental sort of guy, to hell with it. I'll be checkin' in with you during the game. *(Click. They sit. Adjust mics. They assemble their data sheets. Booter and Dazzy both sip at the same time. One with coffee, one with beer. Dazzy does his routine with great sloth and sloppiness. Booter is chipper and methodical. Dazzy finishes his routine. Booter sharpens pencils. Straightens papers. Tests pencils' sharpness. Straightens mic cord. Takes out atomizer. Sprays. Puts it back in a drawer. Does "me-me-me-me." Dazzy slumped with beer, watches. Finished. Booter sits, hands folded on desk. They wait.)*

DAZZY. Yeah. Well.

BOOTER. Yeah. Well.

DAZZY. Last time.

BOOTER. Last time.

DAZZY. No more.

BOOTER. No more.

DAZZY. Are you going to repeat everything I say?

BOOTER. Sorry, Daz.

DAZZY. This is it, Booter.

BOOTER. This is it.

DAZZY. Stop that.

BOOTER. Sorry, Daz.

DAZZY. Seventh game of the World Series.

BOOTER. Bottom of the ninth.

DAZZY. That's better.

BOOTER. Thank you.

DAZZY. Bottom of the ninth.

BOOTER. Bases loaded.

DAZZY. We're at bat.

BOOTER. The scene is set for something memorable.

DAZZY. This is it. Our time.

BOOTER. The last time.

DAZZY. The last time.

BOOTER. The wind-up.

DAZZY. And the pitch...

BOOTER. The batter swings.

DAZZY. A deep line drive to center field.

BOOTER. Willie Mays is going back, going back.

DAZZY. Listen to that crowd. *(Silence. They suspend. Then break. Dazzy sips. Booter does his papers.)* Well, it's been a lotta years.

BOOTER. A lotta years.

DAZZY. A heckuva' lotta years.

BOOTER. A passel of years.

DAZZY. *(pause)* How many years?

BOOTER. I don't know, Daz.

DAZZY. How many years?

BOOTER. *(slight pause)* Twenty-five.

DAZZY. *(pause)* Twenty-five goddam friggin' years.

BOOTER. It's been swell, Daz.

DAZZY. You know what I like about you, Booter?

BOOTER. What, Daz? What do you like about me?

DAZZY. You're the only guy I know outside of old movies who still says "swell." *(Dazzy extends hand. Booter takes it.)* To twenty-five goddam friggin' years.

BOOTER. It's been swell. *(Booter gets a puzzled look on his face.)*

DAZZY. What's the matter?

BOOTER. I wonder if you can say "friggin'" on the air. I'll have to look that up.

DAZZY. What for? This is the last time.

BOOTER. ... Still... It doesn't hurt to look it up. *(Pause. They sip.)* Great day for a ballgame. Sun is shining. Grass is green. Not too hot. It's juu-uust right. *(pause)* Yes, sir. Just a great day for a ballgame.

DAZZY. *(pause)* Twenty-five years and the bastards pull the plug.

BOOTER. *(pause)* Well... All good things must come to an end.

DAZZY. That's a helluva thing to say.

BOOTER. The old must make way for the new.

DAZZY. That's another helluva thing to say. *(pause)* What're you going to do?

BOOTER. Oh, I'll keep busy.

DAZZY. How?

BOOTER. *(pause)* I'll do things.

DAZZY. What?

BOOTER. Lots of things. I'll play golf. Maybe play more golf. Develop hobbies. Like golf. Get to know my wife. Baseball's a tough life for a wife. I'm always on the road. I don't mind. But, well, you know how women are.

DAZZY. Once in Chicago in 1947 I thought I knew how women were. But no more. Now I'm not so sure. I don't know what women today are like. All the women I date look like Adlai Stevenson.

BOOTER. Connie — my beautiful bride — keeps saying we should get to know each other as people. Whatever that means.

DAZZY. Connie?

BOOTER. Yeah. My beautiful bride.

DAZZY. Well... That she is.

BOOTER. So you were saying about Chicago.

DAZZY. You okay?

BOOTER. I'm okay. So about Chicago.

DAZZY. *(pause)* Funny. I remember everything about that room.

BOOTER. What room?

DAZZY. Chicago. 1947... She was a widow. A little older than me. Hell, I was a rookie. She had her bed right by the window. And I could see all the traffic. And I was very impressed by that. All that traffic. The big city. And I'll never forget the way the light came through the window. I probably hadn't been laid more'n a couple times. And I thought to myself. Man, this is livin'. Here I am in bed with a redheaded widow-woman in Chicago pitchin' in the big leagues and I can hear the traffic and everything... And you know, Booter... I loved her. And we lie in bed all morning listening to that traffic and then that afternoon I went out and beat the Chicago Cubs four to nothing. Struck out eleven. That's the last time I knew something about women... Yessir. That was some kinda woman in Chicago.

BOOTER. And then there's my boys. I want to spend time with my boys.

DAZZY. I got news for you, pal, they're at the age they don't want to spend more time with you.

BOOTER. I know.

DAZZY. *(pause)* You like your boys don't you, Booter.

BOOTER. Oh, they're swell. *(pause)* What will you do?

DAZZY. Oh. Go back to Mississippi, go fishing and get fat. That's my new goal. To become the fattest man in Mississippi. Hell, I may get so fat I'll have to live in Louisiana *and* Mississippi. *(They laugh. Dazzy grows serious. Trying to sound off-hand.)* Oh, by the way, are you going to continue announcing?

BOOTER. Oh... No.

DAZZY. Bet you've had offers though.

BOOTER. Oh sure. But it wouldn't be the same without you, Daz.

DAZZY. No, it wouldn't.

BOOTER. You've had offers too, haven't you, Daz?

DAZZY. Oh sure. Sure I have. Plenty.

BOOTER. That's good.

DAZZY. Plenty. But I've had it. Twenty-five goddam friggin' years is enough.

BOOTER. You said it.

DAZZY. I know I said it. I need another beer. *(Dazzy drains his beer and gets a new one from below. Booter writing something.)*

BOOTER. Better go easy on the brewskies. We gotta lotta ballgame to announce. *(Dazzy takes a long swig.)*

DAZZY. Yeah. We gotta lotta ballgame.

BOOTER. *(trying to sound off-hand)* Oh, by the way, Havelmeyer and Kimble are gonna be here soon to help us call the game.

DAZZY. *(darkly)* To help us call the game?

BOOTER. Yeah. Havelmeyer and Kimble.

DAZZY. *(growling)* Havelmeyer...

BOOTER. And Kimble.

DAZZY. *(with control)* But I hate Havelmeyer and Kimble.

BOOTER. I know you do, Daz.

DAZZY. I despise Havelmeyer and Kimble.

BOOTER. I know you do, Daz.

DAZZY. I'd like to grind 'em up into little bits and pieces and scatter 'em over Honus Wagner's grave.

BOOTER. We all would, Daz.

DAZZY. *(exploding)* Then why the hell are they coming to help us?

BOOTER. The network thought it would be a good idea if we introduced them. Since they're gonna take over after we're gone.

DAZZY. I don't want to introduce them.

BOOTER. ... The network thought it'd be a good idea.

DAZZY. The idea's fulla' crap! The network's fulla' crap! The country is fulla' crap! Why wasn't I informed? Who said I'd do it?

BOOTER. I said you'd do it, Daz.

DAZZY. You said I'd do that, did you, Booter?

BOOTER. Yeah, Daz, I did.

DAZZY. Then you're fulla' crap! I ain't gonna do it! I'm not gonna introduce them squeaky clean, cosmeticized, polyesterized, little no-balled bastards. Hell's bells! I'm Ol' Daz! One of the greatest men ever to throw a baseball with his left hand! Hell! I've thrown more horsehide than a whole field of polo ponies! I'm Ol' Daz! They can't drop me like a hot potato and expect me to introduce the guys jerkin' the rug out from under me! Can they? Can they? Hell! I'm Ol' Daz!

BOOTER. *(pause)* The network thought it'd be a good idea, Daz.

DAZZY. What's more, I'm in the Hall of Fame.

BOOTER. I know you are, Daz.

DAZZY. Can't treat a Hall of Famer like that.

BOOTER. I'll do most of the talking if you'll just say a coupla' words.

DAZZY. I'll say a coupla' words, "eat shit."

BOOTER. Daz, I'll handle it. Just say a coupla' *nice* things, just do that for me. Would ya' do that for the Ol' Booter?

DAZZY. Well...

BOOTER. C'mon now. Say, "I'll do it for the Ol' Booter."

DAZZY. Well.

BOOTER. C'mon.

DAZZY. I'll... do it for the Ol' Booter.

BOOTER. Atta' boy, Daz. And don't forget to smile.

DAZZY. Smile?

BOOTER. Yeah. Smile.

DAZZY. You didn't say I had to smile.

BOOTER. Well, Daz — ya gotta smile.

DAZZY. All you said was I had to say a coupla' nice things. You didn't say anything about smiling. Smiling has to be negotiated.

BOOTER. Well, would you smile for the Ol' Booter?

DAZZY. Seems like I'm doin' a lot for the Ol' Booter all of a sudden.

BOOTER. Twenty-five years, Daz.

DAZZY. Okay. Okay. Make me feel guilty why doncha'.

BOOTER. Oh and Daz?

DAZZY. What?

BOOTER. You said I was fulla' crap.

DAZZY. When?

BOOTER. Just now. You said the networks were fulla' crap. The country was fulla' crap and that I was fulla' crap.

DAZZY. Well?

BOOTER. I'm not fulla' crap. Am I?

DAZZY. Hell no. You're the Ol' Booter. *(Pause. Booter ponders. Daz stands, pops open another beer. Sips. Nothing.)* My, how time flies when you're having fun. What happened to all those years when I was young? *(pause)* I've been depressed ever since leaving New York.

BOOTER. Yep.

DAZZY. Seems like everything is played in domes and plastic nowadays.

BOOTER. Thank God for Fenway.

DAZZY. Not many of the old parks left.

BOOTER. Thank God for Wrigley Field.

DAZZY. And there's still Yankee Stadium. The house that Ruth built. I remember seeing the World Series there after my rookie year in St. Louis. I walked out of New York's Pennsylvania Station a hayseed, hat-in-hand, just off the turnip truck. But I had a ticket to Yankee Stadium. I set down my suitcase — I swear it was made of straw — I looked up, and said: New York, ya Big Apple! One day I'm gonna conquer you! I looked down — someone'd stolen my suitcase. It's all the same. Nothing changes... desolate, robbed... I walked up Broadway to Jack Dempsey's bar. I had some cheesecake. Life was good... Last time I was in New York I decided I wanted a piece of cheesecake.

BOOTER. Cheesecake?

DAZZY. Yeah. Sometimes when I get depressed I get a yen for a cheesecake.

BOOTER. *(nostalgically)* With me it's a chocolate malted... Boy, oh boy, just give me a big, frosty chocolate malted.

DAZZY. Anyway...

BOOTER. Man, oh man, that's eating.

DAZZY. ANYWAY.

BOOTER. Sorry.

DAZZY. I walked up Broadway to get a piece of cheesecake at Jack Dempsey's.

BOOTER. I bet you didn't get it.

DAZZY. No, I didn't get my cheesecake at Jack Dempsey's.

BOOTER. They tore Jack Dempsey's down.

DAZZY. I know. So I decided to go to Toots Shor's for a drink.

BOOTER. They tore Toots Shor's down too.

DAZZY. I know. Then I thought about calling up old Eddie Shenley.

BOOTER. Eddie's dead.

DAZZY. It was one of those days when you forget that you're whatever age you are and that Jackie Robinson is still dead and they don't play ball at Ebbets field no more. There I was, walking around big as life, looking at people and all the time I keep hearing Tommy Dorsey playing "Getting Sentimental Over You" and it was eerie. I started singing out loud. I remembered Frankie Sinatra singing at the Paramount about as skinny as a pencil. "Never thought I'd fall, but now I hear love's call, I'm getting sentimental over you." And I started singing out loud. Crooning like Frankie. I started crooning to all the little girls passing by. And for about ten seconds I was eighteen again. *(pause)* Then I caught sight of myself in a store window. A big fat old man singing to the little girls. *(silence)*

BOOTER. Holy bovine, Daz. You were having a bad day.

DAZZY. No kidding.

BOOTER. Sounds like you were having some sort of spiritual crisis.

DAZZY. I was.

BOOTER. Holy bovine. Did you go to Mass?

DAZZY. I'm not Catholic, Booter.

BOOTER. Oh yeah.

DAZZY. No, I did something I haven't done in years.

BOOTER. Holy bovine, Daz, what'd you do?

DAZZY. I bought a dirty magazine, Booter.

BOOTER. Holy bovine, Daz.

DAZZY. Holy bovine is right, Booter.

BOOTER. *(pause)* If you're depressed, if you're having some spiritual crisis, the last thing you wanna do is buy a dirty magazine.

DAZZY. I know.

BOOTER. It's depressing.

DAZZY. I know.

BOOTER. It just makes you feel terrible.

DAZZY. I know.

BOOTER. Do you have it here with you?

DAZZY. It's here in the drawer. *(Daz pulls out the dirty magazine. It's called Ecstasy.)*

BOOTER. That's one of the dirtiest, Daz. *(opening it)* Holy bovine!

DAZZY. You *know* this one?

BOOTER. I found a copy under Booter, Jr.'s bed. He had it under his box of baseball cards. I should've given him a terrible spanking.

DAZZY. Why didn't you?

BOOTER. Well, he's thirty-three.

DAZZY. That old? Why's he still living at home?

BOOTER. He says he hasn't found himself. I don't know why he never leaves the house. Aw, what the hell. He's not a criminal. He's a swell kid, Daz. *(Booter unconsciously picks up the magazine and begins thumbing through it.)* Yes sir, this one's one of the dirtiest... an absolute rag... pure unadulterated filth... oughta' be a law... holy bovine, would you look at that. *(Dazzy looks.)* I can't believe they show that.

DAZZY. Me either.

BOOTER. In our day, Betty Grable was enough.

DAZZY. She had great legs.

BOOTER. Terrific legs. Did you know she was from Missouri?

DAZZY. Who — this girl?

BOOTER. No, Betty Grable. Heck, a girl from Missouri wouldn't do this. Betty Grable was from Missouri. *(Booter puts the magazine away. Pause. Truly sad.)* I can't believe they show that.

DAZZY. Well... they do. *(Both men are embarrassed and slightly disgusted with themselves.)*

BOOTER. Why do you suppose you bought that thing?

DAZZY. I don't know. I knew we were retiring. I knew that was the old ballgame. All she wrote... I felt sad. I wanted to look at young naked women.

BOOTER. But *Ecstasy* magazine?

DAZZY. Make me feel guilty why doncha'.

BOOTER. Why'd ya do it, Daz? Why'd ya buy a filthy, disgusting rag like this?

DAZZY. ... I wanted to see if I remembered what they looked like.

BOOTER. *(slight pause)* Hey! There's an article on *us* in here! Did you know that?

DAZZY. Yeah, but it's not why I bought the book. I bought the book to see what modern women look like. Readin' about me was just the excuse.

BOOTER. And?

DAZZY. And they look *skinny*!

BOOTER. ... Ah, isn't that just like life.

DAZZY. Booter, *everything* is just like life.

BOOTER. Naw, I mean, here ya' get an article written about you, probably doesn't say it right —

DAZZY. It don't.

BOOTER. Probably's a pack of lies —

DAZZY. It is.

BOOTER. And it's in a book so dirty your kids can't even read it.

DAZZY. People don't read books like that, Booter, people look at books like that. Stare at 'em for hours on end till they distort their vision, till they go blind.

BOOTER. I don't want my boys to go blind, Daz.

DAZZY. They won't.

BOOTER. Besides, ya' don't go blind from the book.

DAZZY. Well, of course not.

BOOTER. You go blind from what you do lookin' at the book.

DAZZY. Huh?

BOOTER. My old man told me, "Francis, don't pound your pud too much, otherwise —

DAZZY. "Pound your pud?"

BOOTER. Sure. So I said, "Dad, I don't want to go blind, I'll just do it till I need glasses." Ha-ha-ha. *(pause)* Couldn't resist.

DAZZY. ... Pound your pud?

BOOTER. Sure, "pound your pud," "jerk the turkey," "slam your yammy," "raise the flagpole," "bark the big benny," "shake the salami," "the five finger minuet," "roast the rooster," "shoot the shotgun," "jam the jimmy"—

DAZZY. Okay. Okay. I get it.

BOOTER. "Mary-five-fingers," "are you lonesome tonight," "the midget digit," "oh, baby, oh baby, smack me in the face with a wet sack, mama"—

DAZZY. I get it.

BOOTER. Gee, Brooklyn was a great place to grow up... hey! I was getting pretty pornographic there! I better watch it. This stuff's pornography my mind already. *(Flipping through the magazine.)* Say, this one kinda' reminds me of Davey Crockett.

DAZZY. *(looking)* ... Davey Crockett?

BOOTER. Sure, the hat.

DAZZY. The hat?

BOOTER. Sure, remember he had that big raccoon skin hat? Big furry thing? (They look at the magazine together. Singing.) "Born on a mountaintop in Tennessee, Greenest state in the land of the free, Roamed through the woods till he knew every tree, Kilt him a bar' when he was only three"—

DAZZY. Aw right, aw right. *(Dazzy moves away reflectively. Booter hums. Begins to rip out article.)*

BOOTER. *(softly)* "Davey, Davey Crockett, king of the wild frontier."

DAZZY. *(pause)* I guess that is a pretty dirty magazine.

BOOTER. That's one of the dirtiest.

DAZZY. ... Sometimes I wish I'd remarried after Helen.

BOOTER. Marriage is a wonderful institution.

DAZZY. You're a very lucky man.

BOOTER. I know I am, Daz. I know I am. *(Pause. They return to their ritual behavior. Dazzy suddenly explodes.)*

DAZZY. Goddam that Havelmeyer and Kimble!

BOOTER. *(pause)* If it wasn't them it'd be someone else.

DAZZY. But Havelmeyer and Kimble?

BOOTER. I know.

DAZZY. *(in a low growl)* I'm gonna get so fat I'll bust.

BOOTER. Good for you, Daz.

DAZZY. The thing I hate about Havelmeyer and Kimble is... you know... what is it?

BOOTER. *(sharing the sentiment)* They never played the game.

DAZZY. Right on! They never played the game. How can you be a baseball announcer if you never played the game? *(Silence. They go back to their ritualized behavior.)*

BOOTER. I think I'm gonna get a cabin in the Adirondacks and fish a lot.

DAZZY. *(quietly)* Right on. *(More ritualized behavior. They stop. Stillness. Silence.)* I feel like a man waiting for a fishing squad. *(MARV KIMBLE leans in the doorway.)*

KIMBLE. Hi! You crazy guys! *(Slight pause.)*

DAZZY. Shoot me. Go ahead just shoot me.

KIMBLE. Ha-ha-ha. Gosh, Daz, you just break me up. You're a crazy guy.

BOOTER. Hi, Marv.

KIMBLE. Booter, how you doing?

BOOTER. Fine, Marv, and you?

KIMBLE. Couldn't be better. That Daz. He just cracks me up. What a guy! What a salty character! You know I come in and he says, "Shoot me, go ahead just shoot me." What a great character! They don't make 'em like that anymore! *(Pause. Kimble chuckles.)*

DAZZY. Hey.

KIMBLE. What?

DAZZY. I'm not dead yet.

KIMBLE. *(laughing even harder)* That's what I mean! Things like that! "I'm not dead yet!" Only Ol' Daz would say a thing like that!

DAZZY. Would you quit talking about me in the third person? I ain't Nixon, you know.

KIMBLE. See, that's another thing about Ol' Daz, you wouldn't expect him to come up with a pseudo-intellectual comment like that! You expect rustic wit, cracker-barrel commentary, backwoods wisdom, chatter and raconteurism, but you don't expect an intellectually perceptive comment like the one we just got.

BOOTER. You don't know Daz, Marv. He's a funny guy. But he's about to kill you…

KIMBLE. That's what I love about you, Booter! Self-effacing to a fault. The eternal sidekick. Loyal to your announcing booth buddy. Never the stand-out guy, always the team player.

BOOTER. I didn't hit home runs. I was a shortstop.

KIMBLE. *(pause)* Can I quote you on that?

BOOTER. What?

KIMBLE. That "never-hit-home-runs-I-was-a-shortstop" line?

BOOTER. Well… sure. *(Kimble begins scribbling line in a pocket notebook.)*

KIMBLE. I missed a quote once and the other guy got the Pulitzer.

(HAVELMEYER comes in. Tall, mature, subdued. Almost somber. Nearly funereal.)

HAVELMEYER. Daz. Booter. Marvin.

KIMBLE. Don! Hi, how are you?

HAVELMEYER. *(beginning the great speech)* I come here today with mixed feelings…

KIMBLE. *(interrupting)* Booter just said the most terrific thing. You want to hear it?

HAVELMEYER. Very well. But I'll listen to it with mixed feelings. Because I come here today with mixed feelings.

DAZZY. *(muttering)* ... The fattest man in Mississippi.

KIMBLE. *(ignoring)* He said, "I didn't hit home runs, I was a shortstop." I mean, it's got everything — humility, simplicity, mythic stoicism. We could do a whole pre-game show on the relationship of the non–home run hitting, good fielding, steady-eddy team player. *(turning to Booter)* We have a deal with CBS.

HAVELMEYER. Marvin.

KIMBLE. What, Don?

HAVELMEYER. Be cool.

KIMBLE. Oh. Oh, right.

HAVELMEYER. I come here today with mixed feelings. On one hand, of course, I'm delighted to be joining this great broadcasting family and bringing the American people this great game.

KIMBLE. *(on cue)* But on the other hand—

HAVELMEYER. But on the other hand, I regret the passing of an American tradition — Ol' Daz and Ol' Booter — two of the greatest guys to ever call nine innings of this great game. I can't replace you guys. I just want to, well, call me sentimental, but I'd just like to follow in your great footsteps.

BOOTER. That's good, Don.

DAZZY. Yeah. Terrific.

HAVELMEYER. But in a larger sense, can anyone ever really follow in anyone else's footsteps? In the words of the 16th Century Zen Master, Haykan, "The footstep falls into the river but once. The river flows into the sea. The footstep is forgotten. There is no trace. And yet the water remembers."

DAZZY. What the hell does that mean?

HAVELMEYER. *(pause)* Well, Daz. Booter. Marvin. That's kind of the way I feel about it. The footsteps left by these great men perhaps in time will be untraceable. Forgotten. Washed into that great river of life flowing down into that ocean of eternity. But as long as there are summer fields and barefoot boys with cheeks of tan, wherever the sound of the crack of a bat is still heard, you'll be there. Wherever the sight of a pitcher holding a runner on first still thrills the heart, you'll be there. Wherever they still watch re-runs of Gary Cooper in *Pride of the Yankees* speaking into a microphone, his voice cracked with emotion, knowing he's dying of a dreaded disease, saying, "Today I consider myself the luckiest guy on the face of the earth," you'll be there. *(pause)* No. We're not saying goodbye to Ol' Daz and Ol' Booter. We're just going to say, "play ball." *(Dazzy and Booter look at each other.)*

BOOTER. Thank you, Don. That was... Well, I just don't have words for what that was.

DAZZY. Well, I got words for what it was. That was the biggest piece of—

BOOTER. Daz!

KIMBLE. Isn't that great! Ever the iconoclast! No sentimentality for Ol' Daz. No sir-ee Bob.

HAVELMEYER. He's a great guy, Marv, never forget that.

KIMBLE. I won't, Don. I won't forget that.

HAVELMEYER. By the way, did you get everything? *(Kimble pulls a small tape recorder from his pocket, rewinds and plays back. On tape.)* "I consider myself the luckiest guy on the face of the earth." *(Kimble switches off the recorder.)* Great. We'll use that as part of the pre-game when we get down to field level. I've always found that nine-tenths of spontaneity is preparation. *(to Kimble)* Let's head down. *(They begin to leave. Havelmeyer pauses at the door. He makes a "gun" with his finger and points it at Dazzy. Continuing.)* Catch you guys later. Hear? *(They leave.)*

BOOTER. *(pause)* I don't know why but Havelmeyer reminds me of something.

DAZZY. Yeah... But what?

BOOTER. He reminds me of one of those big plastic hamburger franchises where you only go to eat if you're a kid or you wanna get diarrhea real bad.

DAZZY. C'mon, let's get to work.

BOOTER. *(muttering)* I'll bet I haven't had a good hamburger since the 'fifties. Now hotdogs, I like a good hotdog. Get some mustard... some relish... a little sauerkraut... man, oh, man, that's eating... settle back... watch the ballgame... can't beat it... ya' just can't... no way...

DAZZY. Booter?

BOOTER. Huh, Daz?

DAZZY. One thing.

BOOTER. Shoot, Daz.

DAZZY. I never told you.

BOOTER. Okay.

DAZZY. You mutter.

BOOTER. I what?

DAZZY. You mutter.

BOOTER. Mutter?

DAZZY. To yourself.

BOOTER. When?

DAZZY. All the time.

BOOTER. I mutter?

DAZZY. You mutter.

BOOTER. Huh. I don't mutter. When? When do I mutter?

DAZZY. All the time.

BOOTER. Old men mutter.

DAZZY. You've muttered for years.

BOOTER. How many years?

DAZZY. How many years have we been together?

BOOTER. Twenty-five.

DAZZY. Twenty-five you've muttered.

BOOTER. That's a lot of years.

DAZZY. That's a lot of muttering.

BOOTER. I don't mutter… I don't mutter much. I bet I don't mutter more than the average American.

DAZZY. That's nothing to brag about.

BOOTER. I don't mutter much. I don't.

DAZZY. Well, I'm not complaining.

BOOTER. Old men mutter.

DAZZY. Look, I just thought I'd point it out.

BOOTER. Well, you did.

DAZZY. Constructive criticism.

BOOTER. Okay. Okay.

DAZZY. The muttering doesn't bother me.

BOOTER. *(pause)* Have I started muttering more? Lately?

DAZZY. No. Not more.

BOOTER. Well, that's something anyway.

DAZZY. Truth is, I've grown accustomed to your muttering.

BOOTER. Well, thanks.

DAZZY. I'll miss your muttering. *(Silence. Dazzy drains his beer. Booter begins muttering.)*

BOOTER. So. After twenty-five years to find out you mutter… it doesn't necessarily mean anything… it doesn't mean you're going senile… muttering… just means… you're muttering… everything doesn't have to have a reason… muttering is one of those things… besides I don't think I do mutter… much. *(He realizes he has been muttering. He looks up at Dazzy. Embarrassed. Dazzy shrugs it off.)*

DAZZY. It really doesn't bother me. *(pause)* So.

BOOTER. So.

DAZZY. Last one.

BOOTER. Last one.

DAZZY. *(pause)* Gonna stay in broadcasting?

BOOTER. Oh, I dunno... I've had some offers.

DAZZY. *(insecure)* You have?

BOOTER. Oh, sure. *(pause)* Some pretty good offers. Some pretty good gigs.

DAZZY. Gigs?

BOOTER. That's musician talk.

DAZZY. Oh. Well I got some pretty good "gigs" myself.

BOOTER. *(insecure)* You have?

DAZZY. Oh sure. Say, soon as word was out I was available, they were on my like flies on horseshit.

BOOTER. Really?

DAZZY. Yep. I feel just like horseshit.

BOOTER. Wow... Say, uh, gotta' extra beer in the ice chest?

DAZZY. Yeah, sure, help your — say, I've never known you to drink a beer before doing a game.

BOOTER. First time for everything. *(Booter goes to the ice chest. Takes out a beer. Takes a sip.)* Ahhh...

DAZZY. *(proudly)* "Finest product of the brewmaster's art!"

BOOTER. Boy, that's really bad beer.

DAZZY. *(defensively)* It's not that bad.

BOOTER. "Sir Toby Belch Beer?" Just 'cause you do promotional stuff for 'em and they give you this stuff for free doesn't mean you gotta drink it, does it?

DAZZY. *(belches)* I like it.

BOOTER. *(mumbling, derisively)* Sir Toby Belch Beer.

DAZZY. Hey! They told me it's Shakespeare. Like Falstaff.

ACT I

BOOTER. Shakespeare you chucklehead. Anybody knows Falstaff Beer was named after that town in Arizona.

DAZZY. ... Yeah, I guess you're right. *(pause)* Beautiful day for baseball, huh?

BOOTER. *(simply looking out on the field)* Yeah... yeah it is... wait... What am I supposed to be doing... I was supposed to be doing something... What was it?

DAZZY. I thought you were doing that pre-game interview with Hoagie Cannelloni.

BOOTER. Right! The pre-game. Holy bovine, I gotta get organized.

DAZZY. That's another thing I've never seen you do.

BOOTER. What's that?

DAZZY. Not be organized. You're always organized.

BOOTER. I'm organized! I'm organized!

DAZZY. Who're you interviewing?

BOOTER. I'm interviewing somebody?

DAZZY. Yeah. You're interviewing Hoagie Cannelloni.

BOOTER. Now wait. I know it was a baseball player.

DAZZY. Really? I thought it'd be a brain surgeon.

BOOTER. Naw, just a pitcher.

DAZZY. I'm gonna step out for a minute.

BOOTER. Where?

DAZZY. I'm steppin' out for a minute.

BOOTER. Are you going to have a drink?

DAZZY. I'm just steppin' out for a minute.

BOOTER. Are you sure?

DAZZY. Sure I'm sure.

BOOTER. Daz?

DAZZY. What?

BOOTER. Don't have too much to drink... It's our last one.

DAZZY. Hey, don't worry about me, kid.

BOOTER. Let's go out in style.

DAZZY. ... All right, kid. *(Mike comes on the air.)*

MIKE. Booter! Daz! This is me. *(They immediately snap to.)* Just wanted to see if you were on your toes.

BOOTER. We're on our toes!

DAZZY. *(to Booter)* It's like he can hear what we're thinking.

MIKE. I *can* hear what you're thinking. Now, just 'cause this is the last time doesn't mean we're going to run a loose ship.

BOOTER. Loose lips sink ships.

MIKE. Quiet!

BOOTER. I'm quiet.

MIKE. Now, Booter, you've got your interview with Hoagie Cannelloni — it's a cover interview for our affiliates in case there's a rain delay. Nobody really gives a damn about this interview. So make it brief.

BOOTER. Brief—

MIKE. To the point.

BOOTER. To the point —

MIKE. You don't have to repeat everything I say.

BOOTER. I don't have to repeat everything you say. *(Daz begins to leave.)*

MIKE. Daz! Where do you think you're going?

DAZZY. To get a beer.

MIKE. Okay. Go get a beer. But don't get too drunk.

DAZZY. I won't get too drunk... Just enough to get through this bullshit. *(Daz exits.)*

MIKE. Why can't they just let me do my job... Nobody understands me...

BOOTER. I understand you.

MIKE. No you don't. *(HOAGIE enters.)*

BOOTER. Hoagie, how're ya' doin'?

HOAGIE. What's your story?

BOOTER. We'll just knock this interview out —

HOAGIE. No, I heard out there in the corridor how this is a meaningless interview — no one cares — so let's get it over with.

BOOTER. Hey, Hoag, it's not like you're the only one who's meaningless. I mean, I'm meaningless too.

HOAGIE. Somehow that doesn't make me feel much better.

BOOTER. Somehow I didn't think it would. Okay, we're rolling. We got the mic on... I think we got the mic on... Yeah, we got the mic on. *(begins the interview)* And today for all you fans we've got a real treat for you. One of the game's all-time greats. A great guy and a pal of mine. Hoagie Cannelloni. Hoag, good to have you on the show.

HOAGIE. Thanks, Booter. It's good to be here.

BOOTER. Well, I understand while you were injured this season you and your wife went to Italy and you had an audience with the Pope.

HOAGIE. I sure did. It was a nice little chat.

BOOTER. What'd he say?

HOAGIE. Well, ya' know, he must read the papers a lot, 'cause he said to me, "Hello, Hoagie."

BOOTER. What'd you say?

HOAGIE. I said, "Hello, Pope."

BOOTER. That's just great. Well, it's just about the end of another season and this is your twentieth summer playing ball.

HOAGIE. Yeah, and you can look it up.

BOOTER. Tell me, Hoag, has the game changed?

HOAGIE. Changed? Yeah. I can't get to first base as fast as I used to.

BOOTER. You been in a slump here lately.

HOAGIE. Some people call it that — but what do they know?

BOOTER. Do you do anything different in a slump?

HOAGIE. Yeah, I don't hit.

BOOTER. No, what I meant is do you concentrate more? Do you blame yourself?

HOAGIE. No, I never blame myself when I'm not hitting. I just blame the bat.

BOOTER. I see, ya' blame the bat. What if the slump continues?

HOAGIE. Change bats.

BOOTER. But ya' never think about what you're doing?

HOAGIE. *(dimly)* Yeah, sometimes I think.

BOOTER. What do you think?

HOAGIE. I think, "Geez, I'm not hitting."

BOOTER. Hoag, you've played with some good teams over the years and you've played with some bad teams —

HOAGIE. *(sensitive)* You played with some bad teams yourself too, y'know.

BOOTER. Oh boy! I played with some stinkeroos. Played with the Pirates one year. Man, we were bad! Hey, we were so bad our catcher was Joe Garagiola! So with Cleveland this year you guys had your troubles I guess you could say.

HOAGIE. Yeah, I guess you could say that since we're finishing dead last.

BOOTER. What do you think went wrong?

HOAGIE. Everything, Booter. We made all the wrong mistakes. One of our first mistakes was showing up opening day. We only had two fellers who could pitch anyway and half way through July one of them hurts hisself. And we weren't gettin' the hits like we shoulda', I mean good pitchin' beats good hittin' every time.

BOOTER. I understand you're working with some of the younger players.

HOAGIE. These kids today, I dunno. They complicate the game. You know the game, Booter, like I know the game. Simple. It's a simple game. Guy comes up to me the other day and says, "Hoagie, I'm in a slump. Can't buy a hit." He tells me he keeps hittin' up on the ball.

BOOTER. What'd you tell him?

HOAGIE. Hit down on the ball.

BOOTER. Simple.

HOAGIE. Simple.

BOOTER. I think you'll agree with me though, Hoagie, that the players are better educated today.

HOAGIE. Sure they are! But they've been to more schools. Hey, but I took some good classes, Booter.

BOOTER. Okay, I'll bite. What kind of classes did you take, Hoagie?

HOAGIE. I took a little English, a little math, some science, a few hubcaps, some wheel covers. *(Booter breaks up.)*

BOOTER. That's a good one, Hoag.

HOAGIE. I got you with that one. But truthfully, youth of America, I never did nothin' like that. I was just kiddin' around. *(Hoagie looks up suddenly, startled by something in the sky.)*

BOOTER. What's the matter?

HOAGIE. Aw, nothin'. It's not what I thought it was. It was something else.

BOOTER. Beginning to see things, Hoag? That's a bad thing for an outfielder to admit.

HOAGIE. Nah, it was just a bug or something.

BOOTER. You know, Philip Roth once said—

HOAGIE. Who?

BOOTER. Philip Roth. He's a novelist.

HOAGIE. Oh.

BOOTER. You read novels don't you, Hoag?

HOAGIE. ... Yes and no...

BOOTER. Well, Philip Roth says, "Oh to be a centerfielder, a centerfielder and nothing more!"

HOAGIE. *(defensively)* Oh yeah! Well, it's harder than it looks. What's he know?

BOOTER. He meant it in a nice way, Hoagie.

HOAGIE. Writers — they're full of it. Talkin' about a game they couldn't play on their best day —

BOOTER. *(sensing disaster)* That's fine! Hoagie, just fine! What a card!

HOAGIE. Bunch of pansy-ass bastards that couldn't carry Minnie Minoso's shoes! Or Wally Pipp's or Tony Lazzeri —

BOOTER. That gift of gab is going to get you into trouble one of these days, Hoagie.

HOAGIE. Or Gil McDougald or Campanella, or Carl Furillo —

BOOTER. We've been talking to the all-time great —

HOAGIE. Or Robin Roberts or Ernie Banks or Cool Papa Bell —

BOOTER. Hoagie Cannelloni —

HOAGIE. Or Warren Spahn or Rocky Colavito or Hank Bauer or Bo Belinsky — well, maybe not Bo Belinsky. He was a shithead —

BOOTER. The Booter's Box was brought to you by Sir Toby Belch Beer —

HOAGIE. Terrible stuff!

BOOTER. Remember that name.

HOAGIE. Tommy Heinrich, Bobo Newsom, Nellie Fox, Smokey Burgess, Early Wynn, Lew Burdette, Bobby Shantz...

BOOTER. Toby Belch Beer. "Drink the brew, we'll leave the thinking to you."

HOAGIE. Bob Gibson, Moose Skowron, Wayne Terwilliger —

BOOTER. Wayne Terwilliger! He's awful!

ACT I

HOAGIE. Brooks Robinson, Pepper Martin, Swamp Baby Wilson!

BOOTER. So from the Booter's Box — Swamp Baby Wilson? This is Ol' Booter himself saying so long till next time! Cut! *(pause)*

HOAGIE. Frankie Frisch, Ferris Fain, Ted Kluzewski... *(pause)*

BOOTER. Swamp Baby Wilson? Why'd you do it, Hoagie? You ruined the show.

HOAGIE. Big fructurating deal.

BOOTER. What does "fructurating" mean anyway?

HOAGIE. I think it means sex with a pear.

BOOTER. A pear.

HOAGIE. I'm sorry, it's your last show.

BOOTER. Say — you're right. On the sign-off I said, "So long till next time."

HOAGIE. There isn't going to be a next time.

BOOTER. Yeah... well, the game goes on. It's bigger than any one man.

HOAGIE. They changed it. You're right, they changed the game. It's not the way we used to play it.

BOOTER. A lot more money now.

HOAGIE. Ahhh! A nickel ain't worth a dime anymore.

BOOTER. You want a beer?

HOAGIE. Naw. I might play. *(pause)* Who am I kiddin'? Sure.

BOOTER. *(getting beer from the cooler)* You going to let this be your last season?

HOAGIE. Not my choice.

BOOTER. Well, it happens to us all.

HOAGIE. Oh sure.

BOOTER. Gotta get used to it.

HOAGIE. What?

BOOTER. Being out of baseball. *(pause)*

HOAGIE. I know how I get out of baseball, but how the fuck does baseball get out of me? *(pause)* You know what I mean?

BOOTER. ... Yeah. I know what you mean.

Blackout. The NATIONAL ANTHEM plays. END ACT I.

ACT II

The booth. Daz, Booter, Havelmeyer, Kimble, Hoagie.

KIMBLE. Yanks batting, G. Bob Roberts up. Two outs top of the fifth...

DAZZY. *(singing)* "Just listen to the jingle, the jumble and the roar, as she glides along the woodland to the hills and by the shore. Hear the mighty rush of the engine, hear the lonesome hobos call, while they're travelin' through the jungle on the Wabash Cannonball."

HAVELMEYER. Yeah, that was the Ol' Daz singing the "Wabash Cannonball."

KIMBLE. We're gonna miss that song. We'll miss Ol' Daz. A great guy, a great player, a great memory.

DAZZY. I'm not dead yet, okay?

HAVELMEYER. No, Daz is not dead yet. And yet in a sense he seems dead because he seems larger than life.

BOOTER. *(intensely professional)* Baseball, gentlemen, baseball. Let's just call the game, shall we? Hoagie — you still with us?

HOAGIE. *(coming to the surface)* I'm still here.

HAVELMEYER. *(obviously pissed)* Yes, and you'll all recognize that voice as baseball great Hoagie Cannelloni who's *still* here in the broadcast booth with us.

HOAGIE. Hello America, and all the ships at sea.

HAVELMEYER. Hoagie, you'll remember, would've had a lifetime batting average of over .300 — if he had retired five years ago.

ACT II

KIMBLE. It's always a pleasure to have Hoagie here.

HOAGIE. It's always a pleasure to be had.

HAVELMEYER. Right you are, Marv. But since Hoagie's team *is* playing in the game maybe Ol' Hoagie'd like to be getting back to the old dugout.

HOAGIE. *(bored)* It's a great game. I'm just glad to be a part of it. Even though I'm not.

HAVELMEYER. So we're in the fifth inning. Yanks nothing, Indians nothing.

KIMBLE. *(bored)* And we've got a crackerjack of a pitcher's duel going here.

DAZZY. Really? Where?

HAVELMEYER. Well, the score's nothing to nothing.

DAZZY. That doesn't mean it's a pitcher's duel! Those guys can't pitch and those guys can't hit!

BOOTER. Lotta fans like a high-scoring game.

DAZZY. Lotta fans don't know what the hell they're talking about.

HAVELMEYER. Ha-ha-ha. That's the Ol' Daz we all love! Incorrigible, irrepressible!

DAZZY. Most fans wouldn't know Babe Ruth from Cole Porter.

KIMBLE. Yeah! All that homespun wisdom! All those homespun stories! They broke the mold when they made Ol' Daz.

DAZZY. Yeah. I remember my uncle Emmet used to say to me — words of wisdom I'll never forget. Uncle Emmet said, "Boy, I'd been your daddy if that dog hadn't beat me up those stairs." *(There is a stunned silence.)*

HAVELMEYER. Here's the pitch. Outside. Ball one.

KIMBLE. If you just tuned in we're joined today by Hoagie Cannelloni. The great veteran playing out his twilight years.

HOAGIE. What twilight years?

BOOTER. And of course you're not the only veteran on this ball club, Hoagie. Hoagie? Right, Hoagie?

HOAGIE. You talking to me?

KIMBLE. *(overly dramatic)* And there's a strike on the slider! That low slider drops outta sight like a mouse behind the kitchen sink.

BOOTER. So Hoagie, one of the pitchers on this staff is, of course, the veteran Winny Bumpers.

HOAGIE. Winny's been around a lotta years. 'Course he's old. Hey, I remember when all the guy had goin' for him was talent.

HAVELMEYER. And it's strike two.

KIMBLE. But then you got the pitcher, the kid Showlander. He's got a great future.

HOAGIE. In what?

KIMBLE. Uh, baseball.

HOAGIE. One time around the league they figure out the Emperor ain't wearin' nothin' but a jock strap.

KIMBLE. Uh, Daz — any thoughts on the kid Showlander's future? *(a CRACK of the bat)*

HAVELMEYER. Uh, oh. A long drive to right. He came in with the changeup, it's in the gap — good for a double —

DAZZY. My point in detail.

BOOTER. Yep! Ya just can't fool major league hitters with all fastballs. Right, Daz?

DAZZY. I had a sweet fastball. But you can't throw the fastball past DiMaggio forever. No matter how fast you were, DiMaggio was always faster.

KIMBLE. What'd you used to throw DiMaggio?

DAZZY. My best pitch. Wouldn't you?

KIMBLE. *(painfully crisp)* And so that brings up the kid Fleagle, the shortstop. Batting a blunt .198.

HAVELMEYER. Of course the kid, Fleagle, is being touted for his glove not his bat, Marv.

HOAGIE. Well, Fleagle is a remarkable defensive fielder in the sense he can't field. But he's young. Only twenty-one. In ten years he's got an excellent chance of being thirty-one.

KIMBLE. Fleagle's just a kid. Just a rookie trying to make good here in the last ebbing, fading, desultory days of a season of disappointments for the Indians. You might say they're discontented.

HOAGIE. *(incredulous)* Discontented? When you lose ninety games it's more than discontented. You take it personally.

HAVELMEYER. But there's a personal story underneath this kid Fleagle's struggle to make this team, Marv.

KIMBLE. Right you are, Don. The kid Fleagle's mind has gotta be focused on the tragedy of his sister, Adrianna Fleagle, a Catholic nun working in Africa, who's just been diagnosed as a leper.

HAVELMEYER. And the kid swings. It's a weak grounder to second, Barber comes with it.

KIMBLE. The kid's running his heart out.

HAVELMEYER. Easy play at first.

KIMBLE. The kid Fleagle — doing his darndest with every step he took, his boyish mind obviously preoccupied with leprosy, grounds into the final out of the inning, so we pause for station identification. Don't change that channel, you might be living in a different city. *(Pause. Cut to commercial. Pause. Havelmeyer gives "cut" sign.)*

BOOTER. *(muttering)* Boy, that'd be terrible not to know what city you were in.

HAVELMEYER. Wait a minute, I'm getting something over the headset. *(Havelmeyer gets a call over his headset.)* What's that? Cancellation? Yeah. He's here. Line four. *(Hoagie picks up the phone.)*

HOAGIE. Talk to me. What? What? Yeah. Okay. *(He hangs up.)* What d'ya know? I may get to pinch hit in this here game. Will blunders never cease?

BOOTER. *(concerned)* Hoag. You sure?

DAZZY. You've had a few.

BOOTER. You've had more'n a few.

HOAGIE. I've had more'n a few before.

DAZZY. Hey, this kid throws *hard*.

HOAGIE. Hell. I was once beaned by Hoyt Wilhelm. It was on a Sunday.

KIMBLE. Did it hurt?

HOAGIE. Not 'til Wednesday.

KIMBLE. *(jovially)* Ah, what the heck. What could happen to you the last game of the season? *(Everyone looks at Kimble as if he's sentenced someone to death.)*

HOAGIE. Well, I guess I'll go grab a bat. So long. *(Hoagie exits.)*

DAZZY. Well — we'll never see him again.

BOOTER. Tell me the truth, Havelmeyer.

HAVELMEYER. If I can, I will.

BOOTER. And if you can't?

HAVELMEYER. I'll bullshit you.

BOOTER. Why're we being canned after twenty-five years?

DAZZY. Because we've been on the air for twenty-five years.

BOOTER. That means we got longevity.

DAZZY. That means we're dead.

BOOTER. We're dead?

DAZZY. Nothing's as dead as longevity.

HAVELMEYER. Daz, I'm glad to see you taking this well.

DAZZY. I'm not taking it "well." I'm just taking it.

HAVELMEYER. The thing is — sometimes you guys wander away from the game.

BOOTER. We do not.

KIMBLE. You do too. *(pause)*

HAVELMEYER. Look, you guys were great guys in your day, but the game has changed. Today we're competing with fast-moving games like basketball and football. We've gotta keep the ball moving. There's no time for tangents. Dead air is just that — dead. We can't talk to the dead. We're not talking to vampires here, gentlemen!

BOOTER. I'll never forget the first time I saw a movie starring Dracula. Whoo boy. That was something. That Bela Lugosi. He was one heck of a Hungarian... Lon Chaney, Jr. was good too.

DAZZY. Was Lon Chaney a Hungarian?

BOOTER. No, but he was good too... He was too fat to play Dracula, but what the heck, you can't play all the monsters... But he was a great werewolf.

HAVELMEYER. This is the kind've thing I'm talking about.

BOOTER. What kind've thing?

DAZZY. Yeah, what kind've thing?

HAVELMEYER. Wandering off the subject.

BOOTER. I still think Lon Chaney, Jr. made a helluva werewolf.

HAVELMEYER. Well, of course he made a helluva werewolf—

DAZZY. He was good in "Mice and Men" too.

BOOTER. There you go!

HAVELMEYER. The point is — we're on the air!

DAZZY. We're not on the air. We're on commercial break.

KIMBLE. He's right, Don. We're on commercial break.

HAVELMEYER. Your job is to back me up.

KIMBLE. It is?

HAVELMEYER. You're the back-up guy.

KIMBLE. I am?

HAVELMEYER. Yeah.

KIMBLE. Why?

HAVELMEYER. Because. I'm sexier than you.

KIMBLE. Oh.

HAVELMEYER. Sorry. Didn't mean to break it to you like that.

KIMBLE. ... Who says you're sexier than me?

HAVELMEYER. Opinion polls. Children. Your wife.

KIMBLE. Oh. Well... they ought to know.

BOOTER. At this rate you guys'll never last twenty-five years.

DAZZY. I wanna see 'em last twenty-five minutes.

KIMBLE. What do you mean my wife thinks you're sexy?

HAVELMEYER. It was just a poll they took. A meaningless popularity poll. For gosh sakes, Marv — don't let it eat your soul.

KIMBLE. My soul? No, I wouldn't do that...

BOOTER. And so here we are in the bottom of the fifth, Yanks nothing and the Cleveland Indians nothing and I don't like the looks of those clouds.

KIMBLE. Don't worry about those clouds, Booter. They're way off.

BOOTER. They may be way off, but I don't like the looks of them, Marv.

KIMBLE. I checked with the weather service, Booter.

BOOTER. And?

KIMBLE. I checked with the weather service, Booter.

BOOTER. And?

KIMBLE. There's a negative chance of rain.

DAZZY. What the hell's that supposed to mean?

BOOTER. Yeah — what's a negative chance of rain?

KIMBLE. Well, quite obviously, it means there's less than zero chance of rain.

DAZZY. Hell, you can't have anything less than zero unless it's my bank account.

KIMBLE. "Nothing will come of nothing." Shakespeare said that.

DAZZY. Oh yeah, well, Shakespeare never played in Cleveland.

BOOTER. Anything can happen in Cleveland — but it usually doesn't.

KIMBLE. Well, one thing that's not going to happen is — it's not going to rain.

BOOTER. Oh yeah? Well I've seen it rain out of a clear blue sky.

KIMBLE. You what? When? When did you see it rain out of a clear blue sky?

BOOTER. *(ignoring)* And so it'll be Showlander facing little Danny Stankiewicz.

DAZZY. Tall pitcher, short batter.

BOOTER. Ever notice how when a guy's a little short, like I am, they always call him little? Like "Little Andy Pafko" or "Little Bobby Shantz." Or in this case "Little Danny Stankiewicz"?

DAZZY. What d'ya want people to call him, "Big" Danny Stankiewicz?

BOOTER. No, but they ought to come up with a new nickname.

DAZZY. Like what?

BOOTER. Oh, I dunno. Maybe midget.

DAZZY. You mean like "Midget" Danny Stankiewicz?

BOOTER. Sure, why not?

KIMBLE. Well, for one thing he's not a midget.

HAVELMEYER. That's right, Booter, and this network certainly doesn't endorse slurs against vertically challenged individuals.

BOOTER. What's a vertically challenged individual?

DAZZY. A midget.

BOOTER. Oh. Well, hey, some of the greatest people in the world are midgets. You just don't notice 'em 'cause they're so short.

KIMBLE. And Stankiewicz takes ball one.

BOOTER. Remember the Philip Morris midget?

DAZZY. *(hollering)* "Call for Philip Morris!"

BOOTER. He was a great midget.

HAVELMEYER. Naturally, that wasn't an endorsement for Philip Morris or any of their cancer-causing products.

DAZZY. Hell no! We're just talking about one of the greatest midgets of all time.

BOOTER. I think he was a Munchkin, too. Wasn't he a Munchkin?

DAZZY. I think he was. I think he was a Munchkin.

KIMBLE. And Stankiewicz takes ball two.

BOOTER. Boy, that'd be a rough life being a Munchkin.

DAZZY. Damn right. Hell, havin' them witches' houses fall on you every five minutes.

HAVELMEYER. The point is, Booter, I don't think you meant to make fun of Munchkins. I mean midgets.

BOOTER. Of course not. I love Munchkins.

DAZZY. I love Munchkins too. Munchkins are aces in my book. *(Dazzy begins singing. Booter joins in.)* "Ding dong the witch is dead. Which old witch? The wicked witch. Ding dong the wicked witch is dead!"

BOOTER. "Ding dong the witch is dead. Which old witch? The wicked witch. Ding dong the wicked witch is dead!" *(The boys pause, realizing that maybe they've gone too far.)*

DAZZY. *(sheepishly)* Maybe we oughta' get back to the old ball game?

HAVELMEYER. Maybe that'd be an *excellent* idea. (SOUND—CRACK of the bat.)

BOOTER. And say! Midget Stankiewicz hits one in the hole! They're gonna have to hurry to get the Midget. They'll never get him! They'll never get him! They got him... How do you like that? Holy bovine. Well... I changed my mind before he got there so that doesn't count as an error. But the Midget is out at first. Say, looks like the nickname of "Midget" has stuck with "Midget" Stankiewicz.

KIMBLE. Only because you keep calling him "Midget."

HAVELMEYER. Ah, yes—remember the trouble Randy Newman got into with his song "Short People"?

DAZZY. I loved that song.

BOOTER. I did too. How did it go?

HAVELMEYER. *(desperately)* And the next batter up is Leveldro Tulane.

DAZZY. *(in unison)* "Short people got no reason… Short people got no reason… Short people got no reason to…"

BOOTER. *(in unison)* "Short people got no reason… Short people got no reason… Short people got no reason to…" *(Pause. They've both forgotten the lyric.)*

BOOTER. Lessee, they got no reason to do something…

DAZZY. Lessee, short people got no reason, short people got no reason, short people got no reason to…

KIMBLE. *(bursting)* To live! No reason to live! Short people got no reason to live! None! Nil! Nada! *(pause)*

HAVELMEYER. I'm sorry to hear you say that, Marv.

KIMBLE. No! I didn't mean that. I mean I don't feel that — I was just quoting the lyrics. Because they couldn't remember — they couldn't — so I —

BOOTER. It's okay, Marv.

DAZZY. Sure, Marv. You probably haven't known that many short people.

HAVELMEYER. I'm sure it won't cost you your job.

DAZZY. We hope and pray it doesn't cost you your job.

BOOTER. Sure, the network has a good sense of humor about this sort of thing — once every hundred years or so.

DAZZY. And besides, I'm sure Ol' Don here will go to bat for you.

KIMBLE. I was just, what I was doing was… out of context is all… But it really doesn't matter… We're all kidding here, right. Right?

HAVELMEYER. And it's a strike for Leveldro Tulane.

BOOTER. Lessee, it says here Leveldro Tulane is from Oklahoma… Leveldro's a funny name. Ever heard that name before, Daz?

DAZZY. Hell no. It's a made-up name.

HAVELMEYER. And Leveldro Tulane takes ball one.

KIMBLE. What was that pitch, Ol' Daz?

DAZZY. That was a screwball that didn't quite screw... Reminds me of a dame I knew in Philly once. *(Havelmeyer and Kimble stare in open-mouthed horror. Silence.)*

BOOTER. Y'know I been thinking maybe Leveldro is an Indian name.

DAZZY. What?

BOOTER. Leveldro is from Oklahoma. Maybe Leveldro is an old Indian name. Of course my geography in Oklahoma is terrible.

DAZZY. Well, you don't have to worry about it because it's not an old Indian name.

HAVELMEYER. And Tulane takes a low outsider for ball two.

BOOTER. How do you know it's not an Indian name, Daz?

DAZZY. Because I've seen about every Western movie ever made and not one Indian was named Leveldro.

KIMBLE. *(trying to fit in)* My father used to watch a lotta Westerns. He'd watch Westerns on TV for hours on end. *(chuckling)* Just wasted his whole life watching Westerns on TV.

DAZZY. Hey! Watching Westerns isn't a waste of time! It's American history for chrissakes!

KIMBLE. *(backtracking)* Well, I, uh, agree, but my father knew no shame. I mean he'd watch any kind of Western! He'd watch Westerns with Broderick Crawford or... or... Jeff Chandler.

DAZZY. *(menacing)* I happen to *love* Jeff Chandler.

KIMBLE. Well, it's true that Jeff Chandler *did* play an Indian on more than one occasion.

DAZZY. And not *once* was his name Leveldro.

HAVELMEYER. Strike two on Leveldro Tulane. Tell me something, Marv.

KIMBLE. What is it, Don?

HAVELMEYER. Are you aware that you just referred to Leveldro Tulane — a potential Native American — as an "Indian?"

KIMBLE. *(panicked)* I would never refer to a potential Native American as an Indian, Don.

HAVELMEYER. Well, it so happens that Leveldro Tulane is an African-American, not a potential Native American, Don, but we here at the network believe in political astuteness and ethnic sensitivity and I'm sure you meant nothing by your "Indian ethnicity comment," Marv.

KIMBLE. *(rebounding)* I certainly didn't, Don — *if* I said it. Because, of course, you realize that even though Leveldro Tulane is an African-American given his genetic heritage, he may also be part Native American.

HAVELMEYER. You're right, Marv. He could be part Native American or part Irish-Jewish-Italian American.

DAZZY. *(irritably)* He could also be Mexican-Martian American, but the son-of-a-bitch just struck out.

HAVELMEYER. What?

KIMBLE. What?

DAZZY. Yeah, while you two guys were arguing over who broke the little red school wagon, mighty Leveldro just struck out.

BOOTER. Thing I don't like about Oklahoma… is snakes.

KIMBLE. Snakes.

BOOTER. I hate snakes. Hate 'em.

HAVELMEYER. Okay, I'll bite. Why do you hate 'em.

BOOTER. Because they bite.

KIMBLE. It's a well-known fact that snakes only bite when provoked.

DAZZY. Not true. My first wife was a snake and she'd bite whenever she damn well felt like it.

HAVELMEYER. *(trying to catch him)* Are you comparing your ex-wife to a snake, Ol' Daz?

DAZZY. Hell no! That'd be an insult to the rest of the snakes.

HAVELMEYER. I just wanted you to know that what you're saying could be interpreted as politically incorrect.

DAZZY. I fought in World War Two and voted for Franklin Delano Roosevelt. Top that.

BOOTER. All I'm saying is I hate snakes. I hate snakes crawling over any part of my body.

KIMBLE. Well obviously! Nobody'd like a snake crawling all over their body. Who could *possibly* like a snake crawling all over their body?

BOOTER. Another snake?

DAZZY. That's a good one, Booter!

BOOTER. Yeah, I thought I handled that one pretty good myself.

HAVELMEYER. So who's on first?

DAZZY. What's his name.

KIMBLE. Forget what's his name.

BOOTER. Holy bovine! And the batter's what's his name. Caught it right in the butt. Bean ball.

DAZZY. Who got hit?

BOOTER. What's his name.

DAZZY. Yeah, but who's on first?

BOOTER. What's his name.

DAZZY. That's what I'm saying. It's what's his name.

HAVELMEYER. Who's on first?

DAZZY. What's his name.

KIMBLE. That's what I'd like to know.

BOOTER. *(crack of the bat)* Okay! While you guys were talking that was a single by Dudley Meiers. Now we got two men on base — first and second. Chances, I guess, of a double steal are low if not nil.

KIMBLE. Steal. Cheat. What's the difference?

BOOTER. Ball one from the pitcher.

DAZZY. Back in the old days this would've been a perfect double-steal situation.

BOOTER. But people don't think like we used to think.

DAZZY. Tell my second wife that.

HAVELMEYER. There's a man on first and second.

BOOTER. And that brings Harry Hooper up to bat... and winds, deals, that slow graceful delivery... and... it's a single up the middle! And Rivers comes up with the ball, holds the runner at third. So bases are loaded!

KIMBLE. Now, the bases are loaded... the bases are loaded... now what does that mean to me?

DAZZY. Well, as Satchel Paige once said to me: "When there isn't no room for the in-laws... don't invite nobody over."

KIMBLE. What the hell does that mean?

DAZZY. Damned if I know.

BOOTER. And ball one to the batter, Bailey Richardson. Bases loaded.

KIMBLE. Life is loaded. Loaded against me.

DAZZY. Don't take it personal, Marv. Life is loaded against all of us. *(Crack of the bat.)*

BOOTER. And Richardson lines one to short — Dent goes deep! He snares it! He doubles the runner at third! Then to second! Holy bovine! Triple play! What a play by Dent! You could live for a hundred years and never see a play like that!

KIMBLE. I missed it.

HAVELMEYER. And that's the third out. End of the inning. The score's still Cleveland nothing, New York nothing. But we did see a triple play but thanks to Marv he kinda screwed it up. And now we cut to a few words from your local station. Cut. Gentlemen, it's been delightful, but I'm going to the men's room.

DAZZY. Should I alert the *New York Times*?

KIMBLE. I'll go with you, Don.

HAVELMEYER. Marv. This may come as a shock to you, but I've been going to the men's room by myself for some time now.

KIMBLE. *(defensively)* Well... so have I... except for that one period when I had to wear adult diapers.

HAVELMEYER. No one cares, Marv. *(He exits.)*

KIMBLE. Wait a minute! Wait, Don. Daz, Booter excuse me a sec. There's something I wanna talk to Don about. You guys are the greatest! Because you are the past. Never change. Don! Oh Don! *(He exits. Daz jumps up as if electrified.)*

DAZZY. Whoa! Whoa! Whoa!

BOOTER. Daz, are you gonna throw up? Don't throw up on me. This is a new shirt.

DAZZY. Booter! It just came to me.

BOOTER. What did?

DAZZY. A great idea.

BOOTER. Well, it's about time.

DAZZY. What's *that* supposed to mean?

BOOTER. Well, I've known you for twenty-five years and you haven't had a good idea yet. You've had some illegal ideas... some depraved ideas...

DAZZY. I've had plenty of good ideas!

BOOTER. What about that time you said you could eat a bowling ball standing up?

DAZZY. I was kidding.

BOOTER. Oh... I thought you were serious.

DAZZY. Everyone knew I was kidding. Now just listen.

BOOTER. How many other people thought you were serious?

DAZZY. Just you. Now just listen.

BOOTER. I was the only one.

DAZZY. The only one. Now just listen.

BOOTER. I mean eating a bowling ball standing up.

Act II

DAZZY. That was a joke! Anybody knows you can't eat a bowling ball...

BOOTER. You can't?

DAZZY. Not standing up. Now just listen...

BOOTER. But... maybe sitting down?

DAZZY. Will you just listen!? I've got a plan on how we can go out with dignity.

BOOTER. We're too old for dignity.

DAZZY. Now just listen.

BOOTER. You know the other day I drooled?

DAZZY. Would you please shut up!

BOOTER. Okay. Let's hear this great idea.

DAZZY. Now. What've we got going for ourselves over Havelmeyer and Kimble?

BOOTER. Well, you've got beer and I've got drool.

DAZZY. No, we've got the past.

BOOTER. So?

DAZZY. So? What do people want?

BOOTER. What.

DAZZY. The past. Nostalgia.

BOOTER. Why?

DAZZY. The past is the only thing they remember. I mean nobody likes what we got now.

BOOTER. What do you mean? What we got now?

DAZZY. This! The real world. Nobody could possibly like this crap.

BOOTER. Well, buuut—

DAZZY. But nothing. People think of Ebbets Field as heaven 'cause they ain't never gonna get there.

BOOTER. Well, it was a good place to play ball.

DAZZY. That's not the point! If everybody loved Ebbets Field as much as they *say* they loved Ebbets Field there would still be an Ebbets Field.

BOOTER. Are you saying, rebuild it and they will come?

DAZZY. No. I'm talking about who *we* are. You and me.

BOOTER. Who are we?

DAZZY. We are the past.

BOOTER. Are we defunct?

DAZZY. We are dinosaurs.

BOOTER. I don't wanna be a dinosaur, Daz.

DAZZY. Why not.

BOOTER. They make oil out of dinosaurs. I don't wanna end up in someone's crankcase.

DAZZY. What I'm saying is you need to play with Joe DiMaggio. I once struck out Jackie Robinson. What've Havelmeyer and Kimble ever done?

BOOTER. Well, they've taken our jobs.

DAZZY. But we can fight back.

BOOTER. How?

DAZZY. With the past. We tell more stories about the old days than usual. The way games used to be. When it wasn't a business.

BOOTER. But it was always a business.

DAZZY. Yeah, but people don't want to hear that.

BOOTER. In other words, lie?

DAZZY. No! Humiliate! Humiliate Havelmeyer and Kimble. We undermine everything they say with what we know best. Which was twenty to thirty years ago.

BOOTER. I've never seen this devious side of you, Daz.

DAZZY. You never had to hit my slider, either.

BOOTER. Okay.

DAZZY. Life is about failure.

BOOTER. *(adamantly)* Boy, Casey Stengel wouldn't like to hear you say that, Daz.

DAZZY. Look. If you hit a .300 you're a good hitter, right?

BOOTER. Right.

DAZZY. Right. But that also means the other two-thirds of the time you're a failure. Right?

BOOTER. I've never looked at it that way. I don't want to look at it that way.

DAZZY. All I'm saying is, we are experts on failure!

BOOTER. Failure? Mistakes — yes. Well, granted I made some mistakes —

DAZZY. We made the ultimate mistake.

BOOTER. What's that?

DAZZY. We got old.

BOOTER. Well, I'll never make that mistake again.

DAZZY. But don't you see? We can still beat them at their own game. We're old and they're not! We know the game in a way that they don't! In a way that they never will! Unless they become old farts like us!

BOOTER. Is that the way we wanna go out? A couple of old farts?

DAZZY. It's just a question of how we go out.

BOOTER. Okay. How?

DAZZY. With dignity. What d'ya say, Booter? We go out *our* way, then we go home.

BOOTER. *(out of it)* Home? Connie and I got a beautiful home. In the backyard we gotta lotta trees. Sycamores, I think. Every year they get bigger and bigger. And the squirrels jump from limb to limb... unbelievable... I think I'll go call Connie. *(Booter exits. Daz watches him go. Mike comes on the air.)*

MIKE. Daz? You still there?

DAZZY. All these years that guy has taken care of me. Now I can't take care of him.

MIKE. I wish there was something I could do, Daz, but...

DAZZY. This is our last time around, Mike. We wanna go out our way.

MIKE. I gotta be honest with you, Daz —

DAZZY. Mike! You know, I been seein' the damn lying doctors.

MIKE. I know.

DAZZY. And you know what they say?

MIKE. I do.

DAZZY. Can't you do this for me?

MIKE. I would if I could. But it's Booter. He's in and out. He's uncontrollable. He still thinks Connie's alive.

DAZZY. Mike... don't we all think the best of us is still alive? *(slight pause)*

MIKE. He wouldn't want to go out a buffoon, Daz.

DAZZY. And he won't! I'll take care of him. I used to be a helluva relief pitcher y'know...

MIKE. What d'you want me to do?

DAZZY. Let us call the game the way we see it, feel it.

MIKE. I'll see what I can do, but no promises. Uh-oh. From the monitor I can see Booter coming back to the booth. I'll give you a cue for the commercial. Again. No promises. *(Booter enters.)*

BOOTER. That's funny. Connie wasn't home.

DAZZY. She was probably out watching the squirrels in the backyard.

BOOTER. Squirrels are cute, but if they get in your attic, whoo boy.

DAZZY. Watch it! I can hear Havelmeyer and Kimble coming back. *(From the corridor we hear:)*

KIMBLE. My God, Don! You had an affair with my wife?!

HAVELMEYER. Cool it, Marv. She wasn't that good.

KIMBLE. Not that good!

HAVELMEYER. These guys are *not* going to make me look bad on my first day.

KIMBLE. What about me?

HAVELMEYER. What about you, Marv? (*They enter the booth, Havelmeyer exuding evil confidence.*)

HAVELMEYER. Hello, gentlemen. It's a brand new world. A brand new inning. A brand new ballgame. So let's all sit down and call the ballgame the way it *is*— not the way it *should* be or the way it *was*, but the way it *is*. (*They all sit as if facing a firing squad.*)

DAZZY. (*in Havelmeyer's face*) Nobody knows the way it is unless you were where it was.

HAVELMEYER. Okay. Got it. And we weren't there. Neither was Julius Caesar.

MIKE. Okay you guys. You're back on the air —*now.* (*Sound of the crowd.*)

HAVELMEYER. Okay! We're back on the air. Bottom of the seventh — Indians at bat. Nothing to nothing. End of the inning. Meaningless game.

DAZZY. There's no such thing as a meaningless game. When you get to be my age you'll realize that.

HAVELMEYER. When I get to be your age I'll send you a letter — Pony Express. (*Realizing he's on the air.*) Ha-ha-ha. Just kidding Ol' Daz. Just kidding.

BOOTER. When my father got to be my age — holy bovine! When my father got to be my age he was dead!

KIMBLE. But then again so was Mozart.

BOOTER. I don't care about Mozart. I care about my father. (*singing*) "Casey would waltz with a strawberry blonde and the band played on." My father used to play that song for my mother...

KIMBLE. And that brings up Hoagie Cannelloni.

DAZZY. You had him on the pre-game show, didn't you Booter?

BOOTER. I did?

DAZZY. Yeah! Yeah! You damn well did!

HAVELMEYER. Can't you even remember who was on your own pre-game show, eh, Booter?

DAZZY. Of course he can!

KIMBLE. Ol' Hoagie looked pretty good for a guy that was about to check out—

DAZZY. Check out?

KIMBLE. In baseball I mean.

DAZZY. When you say that—smile. *(Kimble smiles—huge.)*

KIMBLE. Mmmm. You're stepping on my toe, Ol' Daz.

DAZZY. Ol' Daz ain't that old.

BOOTER. *(wistfully)* Y'know, this is one of those beautiful days when it's about to rain but it's still so beautiful and you have no idea how it's gonna come out.

KIMBLE. I keep telling you it's not going to rain!

HAVELMEYER. *(needling)* Forgetting where you are, Booter?

DAZZY. No! He's not! Who's at bat? Hoagie Cannelloni!

HAVELMEYER. Fast ball, right by Hoagie. Didn't even see it.

DAZZY. Hoagie didn't see it because it was fired by youth.

HAVELMEYER. *(needling)* What'd you think, Ol' Daz? Is Hoagie too old? Should he be in there?

DAZZY. Any time a man faces himself—really faces himself—he's risking something. *(Tense pause. Crowd sounds.)*

KIMBLE. *(announcing)* And Hoagie backs away. Looks like he's listening to the crowd.

DAZZY. He's not listening to the crowd. He's listening to his heart.

HAVELMEYER. Probably thrombosis. *(Sound of the crowd.)*

KIMBLE. And your thoughts on the subject, Booter? Do you think Hoagie's wondering if his time is over?

BOOTER. We'd like to be twenty years old again. If only for an afternoon. If only for an hour. *(Pause. Sound of the crowd.)*

HAVELMEYER. And Hoagie digs in...

DAZZY. That's a mistake...

BOOTER. Boy is it ever...

KIMBLE. The pitcher will probably come high and inside, right Daz?

DAZZY. Oh yeah. A kid that strong.

HAVELMEYER. Any advice to Hoagie at this point, Ol' Daz?

DAZZY. Yeah. Duck... Duck real hard.

KIMBLE. And here's the wind up —

BOOTER. Holy Mary —

DAZZY. Mother of God —

HAVELMEYER. And the pitch — *(We hear a complete silence... Then the ball suspended in a supernatural hiss. Then the thud as it hits Hoagie's temple. Then the groan of the crowd.)* And the pitch caught him right in the temple! Hoagie's down! Hoagie's down! Hoagie's down! Hoagie's down!

KIMBLE. He went down like he'd been shot by a sniper!

HAVELMEYER. They gotta crew coming out — the trainers — they got Hoagie on the stretcher — it looks bad.

KIMBLE. He's moving.

HAVELMEYER. Yeah. But it looks bad.

DAZZY. It looks *real* bad.

KIMBLE. Uh-oh. Now he's not moving.

BOOTER. "Angel of God, Hoagie's guardian dear to whom his love commits him here, there, or everywhere. Ever this night and day be at his side, to light and guard, to rule and guide." *(Booter is obviously in his own world.)*

KIMBLE. What's he doing?

HAVELMEYER. Yeah, what's he mumbling about?

DAZZY. He's praying, you idiot.

KIMBLE. Can he do that? Can you pray on the radio?

BOOTER. Faith! You gotta have faith.

HAVELMEYER. It's a tense moment — we're all looking at that stretcher hoping and praying for some signs of life — for a guy that was too old and shouldn't have been in the game in the first place.

DAZZY. Would you shut up.

HAVELMEYER. No, I won't shut up! This is a tragedy! A disgrace! It's worse than a disgrace! It's a farce! The man should never have been playing! *(Booter coming out of it.)*

BOOTER. Say, listen — Hoagie Cannelloni gave a lot to the game! The game owes him something!

HAVELMEYER. *(cool)* The game doesn't owe anybody anything.

KIMBLE. And they're carrying Hoagie off the field.

HAVELMEYER. *(the ghost of Howard Cosell)* And so they're taking him away. Like a fallen warrior on his shield. A dead Viking off to Valhalla. A martyr to time and the almighty dollar.

DAZZY. The almighty dollar?

HAVELMEYER. It's obvious to this reporter that Hoagie stayed around in the big show longer than he should have in order to cash in the big bucks… The game has exacted its toll.

DAZZY. *(trying to contain himself)* The game?! What do you know about the game? You never played the game!

KIMBLE. *(trying to diffuse)* Booter? Your thoughts on the subject?

BOOTER. *(depressed)* I just hope it doesn't rain.

KIMBLE. I'm telling you. There's not a cloud in the sky! *(There is a tremendous clap of thunder.)* What the hell was that?

BOOTER. That's the thing about the weather in Cleveland. If you don't like it, wait a minute, you won't like it then, either. *(A sudden downpour. Torrential rain.)*

KIMBLE. I can't believe it! I've never seen anything like this! It's like a Biblical curse — it's like something out of Noah!

BOOTER. That's Cleveland for you.

HAVELMEYER. Well, they're dragging out the tarps. The umps have given the signs. It's obviously a rain delay and we'll go to station identification.

DAZZY. *(amiably)* Are we off the air, Don?

HAVELMEYER. Yes. Yes, we're off the air, Daz. If you knew anything, if you're not as senile as your Siamese twin here.

DAZZY. *(still smiling)* Don, before I take your head off I'd like to say a few words.

HAVELMEYER. Before you take my what off?

DAZZY. Your head.

HAVELMEYER. I thought you said my head.

DAZZY. I did. Now, you talk about money — you say Hoagie stayed in the game too long because of money. When we started out, guys like Booter, Hoagie and me, we played double-headers for the love of the game.

HAVELMEYER. Right. And you walked ten miles to school in the snow.

DAZZY. I haven't taken off your head yet, that's why you're still talking. Yes, we were professionals. We played the game for money. But you don't do what we did just for money. This baseball game of ours was more than money. More than ego. More than high-fives. It came from someplace deep down. From places you can't even talk about deep down. Where a man lives... and you and your kind wanna come in here and cut it up and chalk it up on a board, or a computer, with stats and statistics, and say this is the baseball game... Well, it ain't. And it won't wash. Things that leave out the human shit don't wash.

HAVELMEYER. *(rising)* This has all been very educational, I'm sure, but —

DAZZY. Sit down, I'm not through with you yet. *(Havelmeyer sits.)* The game was about boundaries. About honor. About honoring those boundaries. Playing by the rules. Three strikes you're out. Not cheating. The umpire's always right... Now stand up.

HAVELMEYER. Huh?

DAZZY. Stand up.

HAVELMEYER. Why?

DAZZY. Because I don't like sluggin' a guy sittin' in a chair.

HAVELMEYER. You're not going to slug me. I've got a contract.

DAZZY. I've got a contract too.

HAVELMEYER. Yeah, but yours has expired.

DAZZY. Not until after the ol' ballgame. Stand up. *(Havelmeyer rises.)*

HAVELMEYER. I'm twenty-five years your junior. You know that don't you?

DAZZY. Yeah. But I got one big advantage.

HAVELMEYER. What's that?

DAZZY. I'm not doing it just for the money. I really wanna beat the hell out of you.

HAVELMEYER. ... Okay... Okay... I'm going to call my agent.

KIMBLE. I'm going to call my agent too.

DAZZY. That will probably be two of the best decisions you ever made.

(Havelmeyer and Kimble go to the door.)

HAVELMEYER. Before I go — I'd like to say —

DAZZY. Don't. *(referring to Kimble)* And take the little squirt with you.

(Kimble and Havelmeyer exit.)

BOOTER. So. It's just you and me and the rain.

DAZZY. Yes.

BOOTER. How long do you think this will last?

DAZZY. Not long. *(The sound of rain.)*

MIKE. *(amiably soothing)* Hi guys. This is Mike. How're ya doin'?

DAZZY. Not bad and you?

MIKE. Listen. I hear you just kicked Marv and Don out of the broadcast booth.

DAZZY. Uh, yeah. That's about the size of it.

MIKE. Well... probably you should've contacted me first.

BOOTER. And the pitch is to Mantle. Swing and miss.

MIKE. Mickey Mantle?

DAZZY. Quiet.

BOOTER. And it's a beautiful day here in Detroit.

MIKE. Detroit?

BOOTER. The sun is shining like it'll never go down.

MIKE. Booter.

DAZZY. Let him alone.

BOOTER. Wilson's pitch is foul tipped. And it's in and out of Freeman's glove. That gives new life for Mick.

MIKE. He's calling a game that's 20 years old.

DAZZY. And doing one helluva job.

MIKE. But it's a game that's gone.

DAZZY. Not to him. Besides, it's a rain delay!

MIKE. It's our jobs, Daz.

DAZZY. It's only a ball game, Mike. Put him on the air.

MIKE. Okay. Daz. Okay. Next week we'll both be back in Tulsa.

BOOTER. Yes, sir. It's a day that's made for baseball. Wilson's studying the Mick. The Mick wants some pine tar for the barrel of his bat. Pepitone tosses it to him. Now he's stepping in. He's digging in. Wilson wheels, deals. It's high outside. Ball three. Three and two.

DAZZY. It's a beautiful day for baseball, Booter.

BOOTER. All over America, Daz. America is still young. Frank Sinatra is still dating Ava Gardner. And so, Wilson prepares to pitch to Mickey Mantle.

DAZZY. How's that outfield looking, Booter?

BOOTER. Helluva outfield, Daz. We got Willie Mays centerfield. That's why they invented the game — Willie Mays.

DAZZY. How's the pitcher doing?

BOOTER. He's doing fine. He's ready to pitch to Mantle. This is a payday pitch… He cocks — he fires — and this is it — it's a hit! It's a hit! Deep to right! Holy bovine, it's a home run… going, going, gone! The Mick has homered in four consecutive games! Maybe he's gonna home run forever!

DAZZY. Maybe we all will.

BOOTER. Holy bovine.

DAZZY. Who's coming to the plate?

BOOTER. Babe Ruth. Look at him. Eating two hot dogs at one time, drinkin' a beer, and checkin' out the babes.

DAZZY. Who's on deck?

BOOTER. Ted Williams. Look. He's spitting at members of the press. God bless him.

DAZZY. Maybe this game'll go on forever.

BOOTER. Maybe it will now. Maybe it will.

DAZZY. Goodnight Enos Slaughter. Wherever you are.

Lights fade.

Crowd noises.

"Take Me Out to the Ballgame."

END OF PLAY

Prop List

Ice chest/cooler
Bottles of beer
Hot dog
Can opener
Three announcer microphones
Empty Styrofoam cups
Coffee cup
Data sheets

Pencils
Pencil sharpener
Atomizer
Ecstasy magazine
Pocket tape recorder
Announcer's headset
Telephone

About the Playwrights

Mark Eisman won the *LA Weekly's* Best Playwright Award for *Shove* at the Road Theater Company, where it played in repertory with his *The Smoke and Ice Follies*. He has had two plays and one screenplay presented at the O'Neill National Playwrights Conference. His plays have been produced and workshopped at various regional theaters including the Magic Theater in San Francisco and Center Stage in Baltimore. *The Guy Upstairs*, which premiered at the Charlotte Repertory Theater, received a nomination for the Best New American Play award of the American Theater Critics Association. *Sightlines* was the first full-length play published in *The Kenyon Review*. *A Passion for Brandy* was produced at the Y.E.S. Festival at Northern Kentucky University. His plays have been presented in the U.S. West Theater Fest at the Denver Center Theatre Company, the Boston Theatre Works Unbound Festival and Charlotte Repertory Theatre's New Play Festival. *Garbo in My Eyes* was workshopped at the Denver Center Theater Company. *Feasting on Cardigans* played at the Midtown International Theater Festival. *Drawing Room* was presented at Dayton Playhouse's FutureFest 2011. He has developed his work during four summer residencies at the New River Dramatists. He has received two daytime Emmy nominations, a New York State playwriting fellowship, a Writers Guild screenwriting fellowship, two Beverly Hills Theater Guild/Julie Harris Playwriting Awards, the Charles MacArthur Fellowship and a playwriting scholarship from Primary Stages theater. *Shove* won Abingdon Theatre's 2007 Christopher Brian Wolk Award for playwriting excellence. Mark was born in Boston, lives in New York, and is a graduate of Northwestern University.

The late **James McLure** was educated by the Jesuits and is a graduate of Southern Methodist University in a graduating class that included Beth Henley, Jack Heifner, Kathy Bates, Patricia Richardson, and Powers Boothe. In the 1970s and early 80s, he was involved in the founding of the Lion Theatre Co. in New York City, which won Obie Awards for its productions of *Kafka's The Trial* and *Music Hall Side Lights*. His plays *Lone Star* and *Pvt. Wars* appeared Off-Broadway in 1980 and have since been performed throughout the U.S.

and the United Kingdom, as well as in Norway, South Africa, and points in between. He collaborated on a screenplay for his plays *Lone Star* and *Laundry and Bourbon* along with Robert Altman, and then later with Walter Hill on a screenplay version of the plays. Other plays include *Thanksgiving, The Day They Shot John Lennon*, and an adaptation of John O'Keeffe's 18th-century comedy *Wild Oats* (moving it to the Old West), which was produced as an official entry for the 1984 Olympics Arts Festival. Other productions include *Drive-In Dreams, Max and Maxie*, and *The Agent*. His screenplay work in Los Angeles includes *The Men's Club* (with Roy Scheider), *Quick* (with Jeff Fahey), *Kingfish* (with John Goodman), and *Sangre* (with Holly Hunter and John Lithgow). Jim was a core playwright member of New River Dramatists from its first year (in 1999); he developed many of his new plays there, including *Iago*, which subsequently premiered at the Alabama Shakespeare Festival.

The late **M. Z. Ribalow** had 24 of his plays receive some 180 productions worldwide, including at Dublin's Abbey Theatre, at the Edinburgh Festival, and numerous times in London and New York. They have won awards in London, New York, and regionally. His work has been published, anthologized and filmed. He also won national awards for his widely published poetry, fiction, and musical lyrics; he co-wrote ten children's books and published articles on sports, music, theatre, literature, film, travel, and chess. In addition to the novel *Peanuts and Crackerjacks* (2011) and the poetry collection *Chasing Ghosts* (2011), he was the co-author of three books on sports and the director of an award-winning sports website. Several of his screenplays have been optioned; he was film columnist for *The Sciences* magazine, and appeared as a film historian on the Discovery Channel and on special feature documentaries of several DVD releases of classic films. He was a co-founder and Artistic Director of New River Dramatists, and hosted New River's radio show at Art On Air online. He was Joseph Papp's production associate at the New York Shakespeare Festival for several years, then founded the American Repertory Company of London, producing two four-play seasons. He was vice-president of the Creative Coalition (of which he was a founder) as well as international arts coordinator of the Global Forum, where he worked with the Dalai Lama, Robert Redford and Mikhail Gorbachev. He was a full-time artist-in-residence at Fordham University, and taught at the William Esper Studio. He died on August 23, 2012.

www.ingramcontent.com/pod-product-compliance
Lightning Source LLC
Chambersburg PA
CBHW032101300426
44116CB00007B/847